OPPORTUNITIES

in

Speech-Language Pathology Careers

REVISED EDITION

PATRICIA LARKINS HICKS

New York Chicago San Francisco Lisbon London Madrid Mexico City
Milan New Delhi San Juan Seoul Singapore Sydney Toronto

Library of Congress Cataloging-in-Publication Data

Hicks, Patricia Larkins.
    Opportunities in speech-language pathology careers / by Patricia Larkins Hicks. —
Rev. ed.
        p.   cm.
    Includes bibliographical references.
    ISBN 0-07-146771-8 (alk. paper)
    1. Speech therapy—Vocational guidance.   I. Title.

RC428.5.L37   2007
616.85'50023—dc22   2006005190

3 4 5 6 7 8 9 10 11 12 13 14 15 16 17 18 19 20   DOC/DOC   0 9

ISBN-13: 978-0-07-146771-1
ISBN-10:   0-07-146771-8

Interior design by Rattray Design

McGraw-Hill books are available at special quantity discounts to use as premiums and sales promotions, or for use in corporate training programs. For more information, please write to the Director of Special Sales, Professional Publishing, McGraw-Hill, Two Penn Plaza, New York, NY 10121-2298. Or contact your local bookstore.

This book is printed on acid-free paper.

Contents

History of the profession. Why speech-language pathologists are needed. Factors fueling growth. Status of personnel and job opportunities. Summary.

Communication disorders. Speech-language pathology services. Supervision. Teaching. Research. Administration. Summary.

FOREWORD

AN OUTSTANDING CHARACTERISTIC of the profession of speech-language pathology is the variety of settings in which the profession can be practiced. Newly accredited professionals who enter this exciting and challenging field have the opportunity to be part of either large, nationally recognized systems or smaller community-related programs, or they can even meet the challenge of developing their own practice. Career opportunities are broad in scope and continue to offer new possibilities through the years due to the nuances of the variety of work settings.

Another positive feature of a career in speech-language pathology is the ever-evolving, up-to-the-minute nature of the areas of practice, research, and populations to be served. For example, the impact of rapidly changing contemporary developments in technology occurring in the world at large has created new tools for the profession to apply toward assessment and intervention methods and procedures for persons with communication disorders. At the same time, improved health care, an emphasis on prevention, and an overall improved quality of life in the population as a whole have allowed our society both to save and to prolong life. Today we see a greater number of infants, accident victims, chronically ill persons, and elderly persons surviving and needing supportive and rehabilitative services in the area of communication.

Such conditions—variety of practice settings and newly emerging areas of practice—provide a continuously demanding and enriching work experience that is both intellectually stimulating and personally rewarding. While offering unlimited options for experiencing new systems of service delivery, new methods of treatment, and a variety of populations to treat, the profession also provides an avenue for channeling energies into a much needed, recognized, and respected service that continues to be required by a large segment of our population—the estimated fifteen million Americans with communication disorders.

Patricia Larkins Hicks has organized this book into progressive steps designed to provide an overview of a career in the profession. The following topics are discussed: history of the profession, scope of practice, employment settings, rewards of the profession, educational preparation, preparing for the workplace, networking, and the future of the profession.

Dr. Hicks presents information designed to assist the reader in determining what the profession is and what opportunities there are for a fulfilling and rewarding career. The material in the book is meant to orient the reader to an exciting profession that offers both a service to society and a rewarding career to the individual.

Peggy S. Williams, Ph.D.
Former Deputy Executive Director
American Speech-Language-Hearing Association

Preface

My interest in speech-language pathology began when I was in the tenth grade. Since then, I have pursued training through the doctoral level and had the opportunity to work in a variety of settings. As a member of the national office staff of the American Speech-Language-Hearing Association, I was able to synthesize my diverse experiences and observe the profession from a broad, comprehensive perspective. It is from that perspective that this book is written.

Most of us take our ability to communicate for granted and do not realize how extremely difficult it is to live a productive life when communication is impaired. Whether it is getting an education, rearing a child, pursuing a romantic relationship, carrying out a job, or socializing at a party—wherever people are gathered, for whatever the purpose, they are communicating. Other than the absolute essentials of air to breathe, water to drink, food to eat, and shelter from the elements, nothing is more vital to humans than the ability to communicate. This book introduces you to a profession that is concerned about human communication and its disorders—speech-language pathology.

Acknowledgments

Pursuing a career in speech-language pathology was the recommendation of my godmother, Josephine Kennedy. I thank her for the wise counsel that has made my life so rewarding and is affording me the opportunity through this publication to make the same recommendation to others.

Once on my career path, I was blessed to have three mentors: Dr. Robert M. Screen, the chair of my undergraduate program at Hampton University; Dr. Daniel S. Beasley, who taught me both at the master's and doctoral levels at Michigan State University and the University of Memphis; and Dr. Peggy S. Williams, who hired me to work at the American Speech-Language-Hearing Association's national office. Each of them in their own way imparted invaluable information that is a part of who I am today. I appreciate the special interest and support they each have given and continue to give me.

I owe all that I am to my greatest teacher, my mother, the late Herlean Devoe Larkins. She provided me with confidence, encouraged me to take risks, shared feedback and constructive criticism when necessary, and most importantly, was always there to support me throughout my career.

It would have been impossible for me to complete this publication without the support of many friends, colleagues, and my family. I extend my deepest appreciation to Gretchen C. Feldmann, who spent countless hours assisting me with the research, reviewing the publication, and giving me feedback. To my goddaughter, who is also a speech-language pathologist, Ruth McCants Locke, I say thank you for your professional feedback. And to my colleagues, Lisa Breakey, Juanita Sims Doty, Vera F. Gutierrez-Clellen, Sandra Holley, Lesley Jernigan, Tom O'Toole, and Orlando Taylor, thanks for your assistance.

And most of all, I say to my husband and soul mate, Dr. Clayton N. Hicks, "You are the best." You checked to make sure I stayed focused and encouraged me throughout this project. Thanks for being my lifetime partner!

1

Pursuing a Career in Speech-Language Pathology

IF YOU ARE interested in a career that will offer you opportunities to help individuals across the life span from diverse cultures, seek employment in a variety of settings, engage in different work, conduct research, mentor and develop future professionals, personally grow, develop professionally, and become a leader, then pursuing a career in speech-language pathology is an option for you.

According to recent employment growth projections in the U.S. Bureau of Labor Statistics' 2002–2003 *Occupational Outlook Handbook*, speech-language pathology is among the hottest professions in the country over the next decade. The profession ranked thirty out of seven hundred of the fastest-growing occupations. According to the Canadian Occupational Projections System, employment for speech-language pathologists is projected to grow at an average of 1.8 percent per year through 2011, which is faster than the average for occupations in British Columbia.

This chapter provides a brief history of the profession, describes why speech-language pathologists are needed, identifies the factors fueling the projected growth, describes the status of personnel available to provide speech-language pathology services, and identifies future job opportunities.

History of the Profession

The beginning of the profession can be traced as far back as the fifth century B.C., when a number of Greek writers reported on the awareness of speech defects and efforts to alleviate them. One such legend describes the Athenian orator Demosthenes shouting at the sea with his mouth full of pebbles in an attempt to cure his stuttering. It is even recorded that the "speech therapist" who advised such treatment was an actor named Satyrus.

The early nineteenth century marked an expansion of knowledge about speech disorders. The primary contributors were physicians and surgeons in France, England, Ireland, Austria, and Germany who published reports on their methods and results for treating individuals with speech problems. Professionals in the United States were primarily followers of the Europeans. Many of these American practitioners had studied abroad and returned to the United States to practice.

It was the second decade of the twentieth century that brought the first intimations of original contribution to the field by Americans. An increasing number of individuals were working as speech correctionists in the public schools, and some were engaged in private practice. At this time there were no established requirements to practice. There were a large number of quacks who, for an appropriately large sum of money, would guarantee a complete cure within a specified time. But the fact that so many were able to maintain a lucrative practice attests to the real need for the development of the profession in America.

Two significant movements emerged in the years around 1920 that increased the growth and stature of the profession. One was the undertaking and publication of scientifically based studies in this area of knowledge. The other was the establishment of courses of study in the treatment of speech disorders in universities. And as the field grew—that is, the number of persons practicing increased and the types of services and settings in which these services were offered expanded—a number of terms were used to define the field. These terms reflected changes and variations in practice, for example, *speech correction, speech therapy,* and *speech pathology.*

Since language is the major means of human communication and disorders of language constitute a significant communication handicap, and because the focus of the field has expanded from speech correction to the broader area of human communication and its disorders, the profession concerned with the development and disorders of human communication is currently recognized as *speech-language pathology.* Similarly those qualified individuals who diagnose, prescribe for, and treat speech and/or language disorders are recognized as *speech-language pathologists.*

Why Speech-Language Pathologists Are Needed

Nearly fifteen million Americans, or one out of every twenty persons, have a speech-language disorder. One out of ten Canadians lives with a serious communication disorder. More specifically:

- Each year eighty thousand Americans develop aphasia, the loss of the ability to use speech and language due to a stroke or head injury.

- There are more than one million persons with aphasia in the United States.
- More than fifteen million Americans have some degree of dysphagia (difficulty swallowing).
- Approximately seven and a half million persons in the United States have trouble using their voices.
- There are more than two million persons in the United States who stutter, one-half of whom are children.
- Nearly six million children under age eighteen have a speech or language disorder.
- More than five million individuals from racial/ethnic multicultural populations have a speech, language, or hearing disorder.
- Speech disorders affect up to 15 percent of preschoolers and 6 percent of children in grades one through twelve.
- Language disorders affect up to 3 percent of the preschool population and approximately 1 percent of the school-age population.
- There are 30,000 Americans who have undergone surgery for laryngeal cancer, and an estimated 12,600 new cases are discovered annually.
- Two million adults, along with an additional two hundred thousand adults and children who have suffered head injuries, have experienced loss in the ability to comprehend and use language because of damage to the brain.

These data clearly indicate that there are many persons who represent diverse cultures and are across the life span—from infants/toddlers to the elderly—who can benefit from the services of a speech-language pathologist.

The ability to communicate is our most human characteristic. Consequently, persons with communication disorders often encounter isolation in vocational, social, emotional, and educational areas. They are often crippled in the everyday acts of communication that make living possible and worthwhile. Speech-language pathologists play a vital role in improving the quality of life for those persons who have difficulty communicating.

Factors Fueling Growth

Speech-language pathology is expected to grow faster than the average annual growth rate through the year 2012. The following factors are fueling the anticipated growth.

- Members of the baby-boom generation are now entering middle age, when the possibility of neurological disorders and associated speech, language, swallowing, and hearing impairments increases.
- Medical advances are improving the survival rate of premature infants, trauma, and stroke victims who may potentially need assessment and some form of intervention services.
- Many states require all newborns to be screened for hearing loss and receive appropriate early intervention services.
- There is growth in elementary and secondary school enrollments, including enrollment of special education students. Federal law guarantees special education and related services to all eligible children with disabilities.
- There is increasing use of contracted services by hospitals, schools, and nursing care facilities.

- There are more job openings because of employment growth and the need to replace those who leave the occupation.
- Today there is greater awareness of the importance of early identification of speech, language, and hearing disorders.
- Professionals in the baby-boomer generation, who are currently in research and higher education positions, will be retiring.
- There may be an increasing number of individuals from multicultural populations who will need services.
- Seniors represent the fastest-growing population in Canada, which may possibly lead to an increase in neurological disorders and associated speech, language, swallowing, and hearing impairments in this population.

Status of Personnel and Job Opportunities

According to the Bureau of Labor Statistics, 93,200 people in the United States held jobs as speech-language pathologists in 2004. About half of the speech-language pathologists (49,250) worked for elementary and secondary schools. Most of the others provided services in clinical settings inside of hospitals (10,030), in nursing homes (3,670), or through home health-care services (2,740). Approximately 12,810 speech-language pathologists worked in offices of other health practitioners. The remainder were spread across various other employment settings.

More than 26,000 additional speech-language pathologists will be needed in the United States to fill the demand between 2002 and 2012—a 27 percent increase in job openings. A total of 49,000 job openings for speech-language pathologists is projected between 2002 and 2012 due to growth and net replacements. The total number of job openings between 2001 and 2011 in Canada is estimated at 1,910, or an average of 190 openings per year. About half of these openings are expected to be due to population and economic growth, and the remaining half will be to replace those who retire.

Currently in the United States there are shortages of qualified speech-language pathologists, especially in the inner city, rural, and less-populated areas. The states with the biggest percentage of job openings more numerous than job seekers are Arizona, California, Connecticut, Georgia, Illinois, Maryland, Minnesota, New Jersey, Tennessee, and Washington.

The *2005 Speech-Language Pathology Health Care Survey* by the American Speech-Language-Hearing Association (ASHA) reported that the largest percentage of unfilled positions were found in pediatric hospitals and home health, where 51 percent and 40 percent, respectively, of respondents indicated one or more speech-language pathology positions were unfilled. About 60 percent of the respondents to the survey stated that job openings were more numerous than job seekers. A similar shortage of speech-language pathologists was also reported in the 2004 ASHA schools survey. Of the school-based speech-language pathologists responding to the survey, 62 percent reported that job openings were more numerous than job seekers.

Additionally, the shortage of special education teachers in the United States now surpasses the shortage of math and science teachers. Ninety-eight percent of school districts report that one of their top priorities is to meet the growing demand for special education teachers who, in accordance with the new Individuals with Disabilities Education Improvement Act (IDEA, 2004), must now meet the standard of "highly qualified." Additionally, 76 percent of states reported shortages for speech-language pathologists providing early intervention services and 85 percent reported shortages for speech-language pathologists providing early childhood special education services.

There are a number of factors affecting personnel shortages. These include the following: more children with disabilities than ever being served in public schools; persons living longer and consequently an increase in chronic health conditions; education for children with disabilities not adequately funded by federal, state, or local governments; focus on cost-containment in health care; cutbacks in funding to higher education, affecting growth and hiring practices of university training programs; dissatisfaction with work conditions (not enough resources provided, excessive caseload size, administrative responsibilities, paperwork); and lack of available candidates.

Employers in both education and health care settings recognize that they must be innovative and develop strategies that will enhance their recruitment and retention practices. Some of the strategies that are currently being utilized to recruit and retain speech-language pathologists include increasing salaries, using sign-on bonuses, providing incentive pay, pooling staff, and using overtime and innovative scheduling. More recently, some employers have begun recruitment efforts using mentoring programs to target high school juniors and seniors.

It is apparent that there are not enough speech-language pathologists currently available to meet the demand. And the demand is growing; hence, there are many persons in need of speech-language pathology services who are not receiving them.

Summary

The ability to communicate effectively is essential and has an impact on the quality of our lives from the infant/toddler to geriatric stages.

Speech-language pathologists are among those professionals who are critical in assisting persons to function optimally so that they can live lives that are rewarding and worthwhile. Although the profession of speech-language pathology has been around for some time, there is still a real need for more persons to enter this profession. The data suggest that there is an increasing demand in both the United States and Canada for speech-language pathology services, and this demand is likely to continue in the next decade. Additionally, there is a shortage of qualified speech-language pathologists in both education and health-care employment settings. Those who pursue a career in speech-language pathology will find that they can work with a diverse group of people in a variety of employment settings. There are endless options and possibilities.

2

SPEECH-LANGUAGE PATHOLOGIST'S SCOPE OF PRACTICE

SPEECH-LANGUAGE PATHOLOGISTS are involved in the prevention, evaluation, and treatment of persons with communication disorders. They evaluate and treat a variety of problems stemming from disease, injury, developmental disabilities, and birth defects. In addition to providing these services, speech-language pathologists refer clients to other professionals; counsel, consult, and instruct the client, family members, friends, and other professionals; supervise colleagues, other professionals, students, and support personnel; teach; conduct research; mentor; establish contractual arrangements with institutions; work as part of an interdisciplinary team; and administer programs in speech-language pathology. This chapter defines communication disorders; presents two case studies as a means of introducing the reader to activities provided by a speech-language pathologist who is engaged in direct service delivery; and describes the activities of speech-language pathologists who are involved in supervision, teaching, research, and administration.

Communication Disorders

A variety of problems are characterized as communication disorders including, but not limited to, delays in speech and language, articulation difficulties, voice disorders, fluency problems, and aphasia. These problems may result in a primary handicapping condition or may be secondary to other handicapping conditions. Additionally, these problems may be developmental or acquired and range in severity from mild to profound. The following definition guidelines were developed in 1993 by the Ad Hoc Committee on Service Delivery in the Schools of the American Speech-Language-Hearing Association (ASHA). The definitions will be described in greater detail later in this chapter.

A speech disorder is an impairment of the articulation of speech sounds, fluency, and/or voice. These impairments are observed in the transmission and use of the oral symbol system.

1. A voice disorder is defined as the abnormal production and/or absence of vocal quality, pitch, loudness, resonance, and/or duration that is inappropriate for an individual's age and/or sex.

2. An articulation disorder is defined as the atypical production of speech sounds characterized by substitutions, omissions, additions, or distortions that may interfere with intelligibility.

3. A fluency disorder is defined as an interruption in the flow of speaking characterized by atypical rate, rhythm, and repetitions in

sounds, syllables, words, and phrases, which may be accompanied by excessive tension, struggle behavior, and secondary mechanisms.

4. A language disorder is the impaired comprehension and/or use of a spoken, written, and/or other symbol system. The disorder may involve: the form of language (phonologic, morphologic, and syntactic systems); the content of language (semantic system); and/or the function of language in communication (pragmatic system) in any combination.

The interrelationship between cognition and language serves as the basis for effective communication. A cognitive impairment can result in a communication breakdown, requiring speech-language intervention to improve functional ability. The ASHA Subcommittee on Language and Cognition Report in 1987 refers to such cognitively based disorders of communication as *cognitive communication impairments*, that is, those communicative disorders that result from deficits in both linguistic and nonlinguistic cognitive processes.

Some individuals' speech and language skills are either temporarily or permanently inadequate to meet their communicative needs. Consequently, these individuals may have to use various techniques, components, and interaction strategies to supplement their communicative skills. This supplemental system is referred to as an *augmentative communication system*.

Swallowing disorders, which are referred to as *dysphagia*, are also disorders that speech-language pathologists treat. Dysphagia is a swallowing disorder characterized by difficulty in oral preparation for the swallow, or in moving material from the mouth to the stomach. Included in this definition are problems in positioning food in the mouth and in the movements of the mouth preceding the swallow, including sucking and chewing.

Speech Disorders

Voice disorders are characterized by inappropriate pitch (too high, too low, never changing, or interrupted by breaks); loudness (too loud or not loud enough); or quality (harsh, hoarse, breathy, or nasal). These problems sometimes exist by themselves but frequently are combined with other voice or speech disorders.

Voice disorders usually are the result of abnormal adjustment and vibrations of the vocal cords and can be impaired, according to professor and clinician Paul Moore, by one or more of the following factors: psychogenic or functional problems, paralyses and joint diseases, trauma and surgical modification, debilitating diseases, and masses that interfere with vibration or glottal closure.

Small growths that result from misusing the voice are known as vocal nodules, nodes, polyps, or contact ulcers. Although smoking has been identified as a cause of cancer of the larynx (voice box), faulty use of the voice is more likely to cause nodules, nodes, polyps, or ulcers.

Many voice problems improve dramatically with the help of a speech-language pathologist. Some problems can profit by a combination of medical or surgical treatment and treatment by a speech-language pathologist. When faulty use of the voice has caused a condition requiring surgery, the help of a speech-language pathologist will still be required to avoid recurrence of the problem. With some conditions, such as cancer of the larynx, surgery may be required and presurgical counseling with a speech-language pathologist may be recommended. Additionally, persons with laryngeal cancer may need to learn how to use a prosthetic device to assist them in communicating once their larynx has been removed. The speech-language pathologist will teach them how to use this device.

Persons who have articulation disorders have difficulty forming specific sounds of speech. These difficulties are usually characterized by: substituting one sound for another ("wabbit" for "rabbit"); omitting a sound ("at" for "hat"); adding an extra sound ("bol-ack" for "black"); and distorting a sound ("shlip" for "slip").

In some instances, structural and neurological deficits may be responsible for the articulation disorder. However, a large number of articulation errors have no obvious physical, structural, or neurological cause. Researcher L. V. McReynolds has looked at a number of variables as possible causes, including intelligence, motor skills, auditory discrimination, auditory memory, socioeconomic status, sex, personality, academic performance, and the arrangement of the individual's teeth. Few of these factors were found to be related to articulation disorders.

Most articulation disorders can be helped regardless of age, but the longer the disorder persists, the harder it is to change. Conditions that may influence progress include hearing ability, condition of the oral structure, frequency with which help is obtained, motivation, and cooperation.

Fluency disorders are interruptions in the flow or rhythm of speech and are characterized by hesitations, repetitions, or prolongations of sounds, syllables, words, or phrases. Fluency disorders are seen in both children and adults. They can be associated with neurological and physical problems, cerebral palsy, epilepsy, and other forms of brain injury. The neurophysiologic fluency disorder involving the omission of letters and syllables is commonly known as *cluttering*.

Sometimes fluency disorders are also observed in the absence of any identifiable neurophysiological problem. These disorders are known as *stuttering*. Stutterers present a wide variety of symptoms, both visible and hidden. For example, many stutterers show a great deal of muscular tension when trying to speak. In addition, secondary behaviors such as facial grimaces, head jerking, or eye blinking may be noticeable.

Researchers George Shames and Cheri Florance reported that there are numerous theories associated with the cause of stuttering. These include theories based upon inheritance, child development, neurosis, and learning and conditioning.

Other speech disorders include oral apraxia, verbal apraxia, anarthria, dysarthria, apraxic-dysarthria, cortical dysarthria, and phonetic disintegration. These are neurologically based disturbances in the selection, sequencing, and coordinated production of speech sounds and are frequently referred to as *motor speech disorders*.

Motor speech productions are influenced by muscle strength, muscle tone, and the timing of muscular contraction. In addition, factors such as motivation, excitement, fear, and fatigue also have an effect on the motor speech system.

Motor speech problems may be the result of stroke, trauma, brain tumors, infection, and inherited or acquired diseases such as myasthenia gravis, multiple sclerosis, Parkinson's disease, and so on. Another researcher, Leonard LaPointe, reported that much remains to be learned about the precise nature, underlying mechanisms, and correction methodologies of all the motor speech disorders.

Language Disorders

Many different types of children may have difficulties acquiring language. According to Laurence Leonard, a professor and clinician in the field, these include children with "specific language impairment," mentally retarded children, children with autistic-like characteristics, children with acquired aphasia, and hearing-impaired children. Differences in the language characteristics shown by the various groups exist. Consequently, these differences also suggest different treatment approaches.

As with other types of communication disorders, there are a number of theories regarding the causes of language disorders in children. Leonard indicates that research has shown that factors considered in the various theories are related to language disorders in one or several groups of children, but not to the extent that they could be considered causes of the problem. Those factors that are most frequently associated with specific language impairment include: the perceptual ability of language-impaired children, their cognitive development, their interaction with other people, and brain damage.

The language disorder most often found in adults is aphasia. *Aphasia* refers to a breakdown in the ability to formulate or to retrieve and to decode the arbitrary symbols of language. Onset is often sudden and may occur without warning to people who have had no history of speech or language problems. It may also occur as a result of head injury, brain tumors, or other neurologic diseases. However, the most common cause is stroke.

Persons with aphasia will have difficulty both understanding what is said to them and expressing their own thoughts. They will also have difficulty reading, writing, gesturing, or using numbers. Their speech may be limited to short phrases or single words, such as names of objects or actions. Frequently, smaller words in their speech are left out so that the sentence is shortened to "key words" like a telegram ("Go home" instead of "I want to go home"). Oftentimes the word order is incorrect or the message is turned around or difficult to understand. For example, the person may call a "table" a "chair."

According to researcher Audrey Holland, recovery from aphasia is influenced by a number of factors including age, extent of damage, location of the damage, and general condition. The natural recovery period is usually from three to six months and is called *spontaneous recovery*. This is the time period during which the most rapid change will take place.

Speech-Language Pathology Services

As the following case studies demonstrate, speech-language pathology services are made up of screening, assessment, and treatment.

- **Case study 1.** A four-year-old child enrolled in Head Start failed the hearing and speech screenings conducted by the speech-language pathologist. A comprehensive assessment was then conducted. The results indicated that the child needed a hearing aid and would benefit from treatment. The long-range goal was to improve auditory, visual, and verbal output to facilitate the child's success in the classroom. In addition to working directly with the child, the speech-language pathologist counseled the family and teachers regarding the hearing loss and its impact on speech-language development and academic performance.
- **Case study 2.** A ninety-three-year-old woman was observed coughing at mealtime. The nursing staff also noticed that she was losing weight and not eating as much as normal. The physician ordered an assessment to determine if there was a swallowing problem. This assessment was to be carried out by a clinical fellow. Since

graduating three months earlier, this was the fellow's first on-the-job assessment. She met with her supervisor to review her plans.

Screening

The purpose of a screening is to identify persons who require further evaluation to determine the presence or absence of a communication or related disorder. In case study 1, the screening was conducted by the speech-language pathologist. In case study 2, the screening was conducted by the nurse during mealtime.

Screenings can be conducted by the speech-language pathologist. These include the following: audiologic, speech-language screening for children and adults, and swallowing. Or the speech-language pathologist may plan, direct, and supervise others in the conduct of screening services.

Assessment

The speech-language pathologist may conduct a comprehensive assessment as described in case study 1 or a specific assessment as described in case study 2. According to the 2004 Preferred Practice Patterns for the Profession of Speech-Language Pathology, there are twenty-one specific assessments that can be conducted by the speech-language pathologist. A description of comprehensive and specific assessments follows.

1. **Comprehensive speech-language assessment.** Procedures for detailed analysis of speech, language, cognitive communication, and/or swallowing function in children and adults.

2. **Communication assessment—infants and toddlers.** Procedures to evaluate strengths and weaknesses of early communication interactions and prespeech–language functioning in infants and toddlers.

3. **Preschool speech-language and communication assessment.** Procedures to evaluate strengths and weaknesses of speech, language, communication, social interaction, and emergent literacy functioning in preschool-age children.

4. **Speech-sound assessment.** Procedures to evaluate articulatory and phonological functioning (strengths and weaknesses) in speech sound discrimination and production.

5. **Speech-language assessment for individuals who are bilingual and/or learning English as an additional language.** Procedures to assess speech-language and communication functioning (strengths and weaknesses) in an individual's first language or a second language.

6. **Spoken and written language assessment—school-age children and adolescents.** Procedures to assess spoken and written language functioning (strengths and weaknesses) in school-age children and adolescents.

7. **Spoken and written language assessment—adults.** Procedures to assess spoken and written language functioning (strengths and weaknesses) in adults.

8. **Augmentative and alternative communication assessment.** Procedures to determine and recommend methods, devices, aids, techniques, symbols, and/or strategies to represent and/or augment spoken and/or written language in ways that optimize communication.

9. **Cognitive-communication assessment.** Procedures to assess cognitive-communication functioning (strengths and weaknesses) in children and adults.
10. **Severe communication impairment assessment.** Procedures to evaluate communication functioning (strengths and weaknesses), including challenging or self-injurious behaviors, in individuals of all ages.
11. **Prosthetic/adaptive device assessment.** Procedures to evaluate, select, and/or dispense a prosthetic/adaptive device to improve functional communication.
12. **Articulation/phonology assessment.** Procedures to assess speech articulation/phonology, delineating strengths, deficits, contributing factors, and implications for functional communication.
13. **Fluency assessment.** Procedures to evaluate aspects of speech fluency (strengths and weaknesses).
14. **Motor speech assessment—adults.** Procedures to evaluate motor speech functioning and disorders (strengths and weaknesses) in adults.
15. **Voice assessment.** Procedures to assess vocal structure and function (strengths and weaknesses).
16. **Resonance and nasal airflow assessment.** Procedures to assess oral, nasal, and velopharyngeal function for speech production (strengths and weaknesses).
17. **Swallowing and feeding assessment—children.** Procedures to evaluate swallowing and feeding function (strengths and weaknesses) in infants, toddlers, and children.
18. **Swallowing function assessment—adults.** Procedures to evaluate the oral, pharyngeal, and related upper-digestive

structure and functions to determine the swallowing function and oropharyngeal/respiratory coordination (strengths and weaknesses).

19. **Assessment of cognitive-communication and/or language abilities associated with auditory processing disorders.** Procedures to assess aspects of auditory processing involved in language development and use (strengths and weaknesses).

20. **Orofacial myofunction assessment.** Procedures to assess orofacial myofunctional functioning (strengths and weaknesses).

21. **Aural rehabilitation assessment.** Procedures to assess the impact of hearing loss on communication functioning (strengths and weaknesses).

Assessments generally involve the use of written and/or oral tests as well as special instrumentation. The speech-language pathologist is expected to document the assessment process and findings. The form of documentation is dependent upon the employment setting and/or funder requirements. As in case study 1, assessments may result in recommendations for intervention. Additionally, there may be recommendations for follow-up or referral for other evaluations or services.

Treatment

The child described in case study 1 was enrolled in a program including preschool speech-language and communication intervention. A description of other interventions can be found in the *2004 Preferred Practice Patterns for the Profession of Speech-Language Pathology.*

Other Services

There are a number of other services that are outlined in the *2004 Preferred Practice Patterns for the Profession of Speech-Language Pathology* that are performed by the speech-language pathologist. For example, in case study 1, the speech-language pathologist provided counseling. A description of other services follows.

- **Counseling.** This provides individuals, family/caregivers, and other relevant persons with information and support about communication and/or swallowing disorders to help them develop the problem-solving strategies that enhance the (re)habilitation process.
- **Follow-up.** These are procedures that are used to complete or supplement an assessment, monitor progress during intervention, and/or determine status after screening, assessment, intervention, or discharge.
- **Consultation.** This is a service related to speech-language, communication, and swallowing issues that includes collaborating with other professionals, family/caregivers, and patients/clients; working with individuals in business, industry, education, and other public and private agencies; engaging in program development, supervision, and evaluation activities; or providing expert testimony.
- **Prevention.** These services are designed to avoid communication or swallowing disorders, minimize their effects, and facilitate normal development.
- **Elective communication modification.** These services are for individuals who do not have a communication disorder but who wish assistance from a speech-language pathologist to enhance their communication effectiveness. These services may include instruction in public speaking, accent modification, or interpersonal communication skills.

As in case study 2, speech-language pathologists may assume roles other than direct-care service provider. They may be supervisors, teachers, researchers, or administrators. A description of these roles follows.

Supervision

Speech-language pathologists supervise professional colleagues, students, clinical fellows, and support personnel through observation, conferences, review of records, and other procedures. Supervision primarily involves the tasks and skills of "clinical teaching" related to the interaction between a clinician and client.

Teaching

The role of the speech-language pathologist in the college or university is very similar to that of other college professors. In addition to lecturing in the classroom, the college faculty member may see clients, supervise students who are learning to work with persons who have communication disorders, and/or conduct research.

Another type of teaching is found in special classes for children with communication and learning disabilities. Small classes of children who have severe learning problems associated with impairments in their communication processes may be taught by speech-language pathologists.

Research

Speech-language pathologists may spend their time investigating various aspects of the processes of human communication. The

American Speech-Language-Hearing Association identifies three basic categories of research activities:

1. Conduct basic research to better understand the physical, psychological, and social factors underlying normal communication.
2. Conduct applied research for the purpose of trying new procedures or technologies to find better ways of identifying and treating persons with communication and related disorders.
3. Collaborate with engineers, physicians, dentists, and educators to adapt or develop technology so children can function more effectively in school, at work, and in social settings.

Administration

Speech-language pathologists who assume roles in administration find their responsibilities to include employing personnel, obtaining funds to operate programs, ensuring that the physical plant is adequate to the needs of the program and patients, evaluating employee performance, writing reports on the operation of the program, and improving the quality of services provided. The administrator works with many persons and agencies to carry out these responsibilities.

Summary

Speech-language pathologists may assume a variety of roles including direct service provider, supervisor, teacher, researcher, coach, mentor, and/or administrator. Given the role, speech-language pathologists also engage in an assortment of activities. There is a multiplicity of options accessible for persons pursuing a career in speech-language pathology. This makes for a stimulating career—one that fosters personal growth and development.

3

Employment Settings

Speech-language pathologists are employed in a variety of settings including:

Adult day-care centers
Colleges and universities
Community speech and hearing centers
Federal uniformed services
Health maintenance organizations
Home health agencies
Hospitals
Long-term care facilities
Private practices
Public and private schools
Research laboratories/agencies
Residential facilities

State and federal agencies
State and local health departments

This chapter provides a demographic profile of primary employment settings of speech-language pathologists and a general description of the varied settings.

Demographic Profile

The American Speech-Language-Hearing Association (ASHA) conducted a demographic profile of its 118,437 members in 2004. Table 3.1 provides a breakdown of ASHA members by primary employment setting. These data suggest that the majority of ASHA members (54.5 percent) are employed in education facilities (schools, colleges, and universities). Members indicated that health-care facilities are the second primary employment setting (39.6 percent), including hospitals and residential facilities. Nonresidential health-care facilities ranked third (17.3 percent), including home health, private practice, speech and hearing centers, private physician's offices, and other nonresidential facilities.

These counts include persons who were ASHA members, nonmember certificate holders, or international affiliates during the period and whose dues/fees were paid. The percentages are for the number of respondents to that question only; percentages may not total 100 percent due to rounding.

Following the table are descriptions of the various settings in which speech-language pathologists are employed. They have been adapted from *Delivery of Speech-Language Pathology and Audiology Services* by Richard M. Flower.

Table 3.1 Profile of ASHA Members by Primary Employment Setting

Educational Facilities (59.2%)

Setting	Percent Employed
Special School	2.3%
Preschool	9.5%
Elementary School	25.5%
Secondary School	3.1%
Several Schools	13.9%
Schools (Unspecified)	1.2%
College/University	3.7%

Health-Care Facilities (35.5%)

Setting	Percent Employed
Hospital Facility	14.1%
Residential Health-Care Facility	7.8%
• Skilled Nursing Facility	6.6%
• Other Residential Facility	1.2%
Nonresidential Health Care Facility	13.6%
• Home Health	4.5%
• Private Physician's Office	0.2%
• SLP's or AUD's Office	3.8%
• Speech and Hearing Center	2.2%
• Other Nonresidential Facility	2.9%

Other Facilities (5.4%)

Setting	Percent Employed
All Other Facilities	5.4%

Adapted from ASHA's demographic profile of its member and nonmember certificate holders in speech-language pathology for January 1 through December 31, 2005.

Adult Day Health-Care Centers

These centers serve clients who require long-term care or treatment but are maintained at home or in minimal-care settings at night and on weekends. The profiles of the clients served are similar to those in extended-care facilities, except that they are more independent.

Day health-care centers represent optimal settings for speech-language pathologists to develop communication improvement and maintenance groups for clients who are not appropriate candidates for individual speech and language treatment.

To identify potential employment opportunities, go to the following website: www.carepathways.com.

Colleges and Universities

Opportunities exist for teaching, research, and clinical supervision. These institutions may also allow you to work with a variety of clients in the university core clinical facility and/or its affiliated health-care facility.

This setting also provides practicum opportunities for students. Because academic schedules must be adhered to, continuity of care is frequently interrupted. Fee schedules vary and often depend upon the client's ability to pay.

Community Centers

Community centers are independent, freestanding programs that generally derive support from individual benefactors, private foundations, local campaigns, and fees. Many community centers are affiliated with universities or housed within large medical centers.

They provide for centralization of services within a single, usually separate facility. Typically, community speech and hearing centers provide the broadest possible range of speech-language pathology services.

To locate centers that might provide employment opportunities, refer to the yellow pages in your local telephone directory.

Day Treatment and Care Centers

These programs accommodate limited numbers of clients; therefore speech-language pathologists are not usually employed on a full-time basis. Clients seen in these centers are generally mentally ill and developmentally disabled. Consequently, they are usually maintained at home or in small residential units.

Federal Uniformed Services

Speech-language pathologists provide clinical services and conduct research for the U.S. Air Force, Army, Navy, and the Public Health Service. To obtain information about potential employment opportunities, visit the U.S. Public Health Service Recruitment website at www.usphs.gov.

Health Maintenance Organizations

Health Maintenance Organizations (HMOs) are comprehensive health-care financing and delivery organizations that provide or arrange for provision of health-care services to enrollees within a geographical area through a panel of providers. HMOs contract with or directly employ participating health-care providers, and these include speech-language pathologists. HMO members are required to choose from among these providers for all of their health-care services. Services are provided on an inpatient or outpatient basis.

High-Risk Infant Programs

Children from birth to three years of age are generally seen in high-risk infant programs. They may be sponsored by public agencies or by various private, nonprofit community agencies. Services are provided by a team of professionals either within a center or at the client's home.

Home-Health Agencies

Two different client groups are served by home-health agencies: individuals discharged from acute or long-term inpatient facilities who still require care but cannot obtain it on an outpatient basis; and individuals with severe irremediable deficits or with progressive chronic diseases.

Speech-language pathologists are employed in this setting either on a full-time or part-time basis. To identify potential employment opportunities, visit the following websites: www.tlcathome.com and www.carepathways.com.

Hospices

A hospice is a public agency or private organization that provides supportive care for the terminally ill in a homelike setting. Services are available on a twenty-four-hour basis.

To identify potential employment opportunities, you can visit the American Academy of Hospice and Palliative Medicine website at www.aahpm.org.

Hospitals

These facilities may provide services for patients of all ages, and some, such as children's hospitals or hospitals for military or veteran personnel, may house specialized populations. Acute care, rehabilitation, and psychiatric hospitals may offer speech-language pathology services on an inpatient/outpatient basis. According to the American Hospital Association's 2004 annual survey, the total number of all registered hospitals in the United States is 5,759.

To obtain information online about employment opportunities in this setting, visit the following websites: www.hospitallink.com, www.healthjobsusa.com, and www.aha.org.

Mobile Health Clinics

Mobile health clinics are specially equipped trailers or vans that are usually under the auspices of state or local health departments, school districts, or various community agencies. These clinics provide services to industries, public schools, or other community groups. Clients who are hard to reach or do not have access to more traditional health-care facilities benefit from this type of clinic.

Nursing Homes

According to the American Health Care Association, there are approximately sixteen thousand nursing facilities. Freestanding and single-function nursing homes are disappearing. In their places are campuses for serving the elderly in housing and nursing homes and in continuing-care retirement communities, which offer a vast array of services. The modern nursing home offers inpatient, outpatient, and outreach services.

Nursing facilities represent a significant segment of the rehabilitation industry, and it is likely that many more skilled nursing facilities will establish rehabilitation programs in the future in response to the demand from third-party payers for less costly nonhospital-based care. Many nursing facilities already provide rehabilitation services. Speech-language pathologists are employed directly by the facility or provide services on a contractual basis. To obtain information about industry trends and potential employment opportunities in nursing facilities, you can visit the American Health Care Association website at www.ahca.org.

Private Practice

In private practice, services are delivered for profit. A contract is established directly between the service provider and the client. Services may be delivered to individual clients, organizations, or other facilities.

According to the ASHA, a private practice is defined as one in which a speech-language pathologist and/or audiologist, singly or in affiliation with one or more individuals: (1) has total ethical, professional, and administrative control of the practice; (2) has total financial and legal responsibility and liability for the practice; (3) is self-employed—that is, not an employee of an individual, organization, agency, or other entity providing clinical or consultative services unless also the owner of that organization or entity (This condition will be met and holds as much voting power as any other member of the board, even though the practitioner may not hold stock in the entity.); and (4) accepts referrals from multiple sources, and these referrals may include those obtained through independent contractor arrangements.

Public Health Departments

Services provided by public health departments vary depending upon the nature and scope of the geographical area concerned. The department assumes responsibility for school health programs and sponsors diagnostic clinics to serve multiply handicapped clients. Speech-language pathology services are provided in three general ways:

1. Speech-language pathologists provide consultative services to various agencies.
2. Services are provided for needy clients either by a payment for fees for services or on a contractual basis.
3. Direct services are provided to clients.

The extent to which these services are provided varies; in fact, some health departments provide none of these services.

Public and Private Schools

In the school setting, services are provided in transition or integration classes, resource rooms, special classes, and regular classes. Additionally, itinerant and hospital/homebound services are provided. Multidisciplinary assessment services and diagnostic centers are established. Speech-language pathologists collaborate with other professionals and parents to facilitate a student's communication and learning in an educational environment; serve on program planning and teacher assistance teams; and develop Individualized Education Plans (IEPs) and Individualized Family Service Plans (IFSPs).

Rehabilitation Centers

These centers serve a wide range of clients of varying severity levels. Their goal is to enable clients to achieve functional independence. Services are provided by a variety of disciplines. Some rehabilitation centers provide services to both inpatients and outpatients. Support is often provided by government programs.

Clients seen in rehabilitation centers generally present serious disabilities. Speech-language services are provided on an intensive basis. The goal is to achieve maximum rehabilitation in the shortest possible time.

Research Agencies

Speech-language pathologists interested primarily in research will work in settings such as the National Institutes of Health and the Bell Laboratories. To obtain additional information about employment opportunities at either of these organizations, visit their websites: www.jobs.nih.gov and www.bell-labs.com.

Other Services

Over the past ten years, a number of health-care corporations have established contract services, and they have subsequently hired speech-language pathologists as employees. These organizations obtain contracts for rehabilitation services with facilities (such as hospitals, nursing homes, schools, and so forth) and then assign their employees to provide the rehabilitation services. In some instances, these companies may place their employees on temporary assignments in different communities. These types of organizations are referred to as *traveling therapy companies*. Persons who like to travel may wish to be employed by such an organization. For example, an employee might work in a hospital in Tampa, Florida, for thirteen weeks and then in a nursing home in Washington, DC, for ten weeks.

These contract organizations often advertise in the *ASHA Leader* and in the *ADVANCE for Speech-Language Pathologists* publications.

Summary

The roles and responsibilities of the speech-language pathologist will vary depending upon the employment setting. Trends suggest that an increasing amount of work will be available in school-based, bilingual, private-practice, and corporate settings. Additionally, the type of persons to be served will differ. These differences may be attributed to the following characteristics: age, gender, ethnicity, type and severity of the communication disorder, and functional communication status. You can develop a long-term career within one employment setting or choose to diversify your career by practicing in multiple settings. Regardless of your choice, a career in speech-language pathology offers you flexibility.

4

REWARDS OF THE PROFESSION

PURSUING A CAREER in speech-language pathology offers both personal and financial rewards. These often vary depending upon career choices. However, there is one benefit that is consistent, irrespective of what you choose to do; there is personal satisfaction derived from serving others.

This chapter discusses the personal rewards from the perspective of speech-language pathologists who have made different career choices. Financial rewards are described based on employment settings; the speech language pathologist's credentials, education, and years of experience; and the region of the country where employed.

Personal Rewards

Speech-language pathology offers many opportunities to individuals interested in providing services to persons who are communicatively impaired. The profession demands that speech-language pathologists continuously strive to improve their skills, identify new procedures and products, penetrate unexplored processes underlying human communicative behavior, and develop and refine educational, research, and service programs. Working to achieve these and participating in the advancement and growth of the profession provide rich sources of personal satisfaction. Following are personal examples of the rewards that have been derived from individuals who chose to pursue a career in speech-language pathology.

Lesley Jernigan, director of a community speech and hearing center, cites "personal satisfaction from having an impact on the quality of life of someone who had a need" as his reward. This translates into a "good feeling" because a person has been measurably helped and can experience the joy of communicating. Jernigan indicates that although the financial benefits have been good, it is the feeling of having made a difference in someone's life that has been the most rewarding.

After more than thirty years, Lisa Breakey, a private practitioner in California, continues to feel excited about her career as a speech-language pathologist. She likes having the opportunity to change—being able to do a variety of things. And that is what she has done: practiced as a clinician, conducted research, taught in a university, worked as an administrator, established a private practice, and served as a leader in her professional association, to name just a few. Consequently, she points out, all the knowledge and skills she gained while in graduate training have been put to use.

Tom O'Toole, a Maryland-based consultant, thinks the preparation required of speech-language pathologists provides a twofold benefit: you can practice as a speech-language pathologist, and those same skills afford you the opportunity to pursue other professional opportunities related to and outside of the profession. For example, his experience in the public schools afforded him the opportunity to make the move from a practicing clinician to an administrator of special education. Another example involved a colleague who moved on to become the principal of a public school. The opportunity to meet and work with interesting, dedicated, and exciting people is what has been most rewarding for O'Toole.

Sandra Holley, the dean of the School of Graduate Studies at Southern Connecticut State University, found her personal rewards in the development of her students and in the opportunity to continue to make innovations in her training program. Over the years, Holley's students have graduated and moved on to pursue career paths in many directions, from working in the schools to establishing profitable private practices. Additionally, because of a grant awarded her from the U.S. Department of Education, Holley was able to mentor a cadre of minority students.

Holley was elected the first African-American president of the American Speech-Language-Hearing Association. During her leadership, she facilitated the association's focus on multicultural issues, launched its public relations campaign, and revised its bylaws. Although these accomplishments were rewarding, she still found the time she spent as president meeting with graduate and undergraduate students throughout the country the most rewarding. For Holley, mentoring and developing future professionals is what she sees as the most important aspect of her career. In her words, "My students are my legacy."

Vera F. Gutierrez-Clellen was drawn to speech-language pathology because she wanted to help individuals with special needs, provide a valuable human service to the community, and work as an independent professional. Because her focus is to develop assessment instruments and intervention goals that can help bilingual children with language disorders, her work has a direct impact on improving the lives of these children and their families. Gutierrez-Clellen says the rewards multiply exponentially!

In high school, Juanita Doty's teacher gave her a book that described a speech therapist helping people communicate effectively. That provided Doty with an inspiration to help those in need. Most of her work in the profession has been with children in Head Start. She has consulted across her home state, Mississippi, and across the nation.

When Doty was director of a university speech and hearing center, she often told her students, "What you get out of the profession is based on what you put in." And Doty has put much in—long hours, lots of energy, and a commitment to help others. She has served on many ASHA committees and as chair of the board of directors, National Black Association for Speech-Language and Hearing (NBASLH). Currently she is the senior advisor for outreach at the National Institute of Child Health and Human Development.

Fascinated with words, speaking, language, and variety, Orlando Taylor at age fifteen knew he wanted to pursue a career in communication. He started out in Chattanooga, Tennessee, with a two-hour radio talk show, "Teen Time," and got enormous ratings at a time when it was rare to find an African-American on the radio. He went off to Hampton University (Institute), Hampton, Virginia, where he met a fellow student who introduced him to speech correction. And since he also had a fascination with being a humanitarian, this field provided him an opportunity to explore communication and at the same time help others.

Taylor went on to earn his doctor of philosophy degree at Indiana University. After graduation he began to work with persons with mental retardation, and that led him to explore the brain and its relationship to language. This in turn led him to his exploration of neurology and neurolinguistics. While working with foreign students, primarily from Brazil, he became interested in the relationship of language to culture and sociolinguistics.

Taylor describes his reward for pursuing a speech-language pathology career as the opportunity to expand horizons. It opened up a broader career pathway and facilitated opening eclectic doors to connected professions. As a result, over the last ten years he has provided leadership in fields other than speech-language pathology. These include sociolinguistics, journalism, radio-television-film, and speech communication. Similarly he has provided leadership at the department chair, dean, and vice president levels at Howard University in Washington, DC.

He was awarded the highest honor given by the American Speech-Language-Hearing Association for his outstanding contributions to the profession when he was awarded the Honors of the Association. He certainly has made a difference!

Financial Rewards

Financial rewards will vary depending upon employment setting, employment function, geographical location, highest degree, certification status, and years of experience.

Employment Setting

The median annual salaries paid to certified, school-based speech-language pathologists have increased over the past five years for both the academic (nine to ten months) and calendar (eleven to twelve months) year basis. The basic mean salaries for the academic year rose from $40,000 in 1999 to $50,000 in 2004, and for the calendar year from $41,000 in 1999 to $54,000 in 2004.

Similarly, the median annual salaries paid to certified speech-language pathologists in hospitals, residential health-care, and nonresidential health-care facilities have increased over the past five years. In hospital facilities, the salaries have increased by $7,000. In 1999, the basic median annual salary was $45,000 as compared to $52,000 in 2003. In both residential and nonresidential health-care facilities, salaries increased by $10,300 from 1999 to 2003. In residential health-care facilities, the basic median annual salary was $52,300 in 1999 as compared with $62,000 in 2003. In nonresidential health-care facilities, the basic median annual salary was $39,700 in 1999 as compared with $50,000 in 2003.

Employment Function

Three of every four (78 percent) respondents who worked full-time and reported an annual salary in the ASHA Omnibus Survey indicated that their primary employment function was clinical service provider. The median calendar year salary for speech-language pathology clinical service providers was $48,000, as compared with the median salary of $64,000 reported by supervisors.

Geographic Location

For speech-language pathologists employed in the western region (Alaska, Arizona, California, Colorado, Hawaii, Idaho, Montana, Nevada, New Mexico, Oregon, Utah, Washington, and Wyoming), the median salary on a calendar year was the highest in 2003 at $60,000. The midwestern region (Illinois, Indiana, Iowa, Kansas, Michigan, Minnesota, Nebraska, North Dakota, Ohio, South Dakota, Wisconsin) was second in median salary on a calendar year at $57,000.

The median salary in 2003 on an academic year basis was highest in the northeast region (Connecticut, Maine, Massachusetts, New Hampshire, New Jersey, New York, Pennsylvania, Rhode Island, Vermont) at $54,000 followed by the western region at $48,000.

The median salary in 2003 on an academic year basis in the southern region (Alabama, Arkansas, Delaware, District of Columbia, Florida, Georgia, Kentucky, Louisiana, Maryland, Mississippi, North Carolina, Oklahoma, South Carolina, Tennessee, Texas, Virginia, and West Virginia) was $41,000 as compared with $52,000 on a calendar year.

The results of the Canadian Association of Speech-Language Pathologists and Audiologists 2003 salary survey indicate that the average annual salary was $59,360. With regard to regions, the following salaries were reported:

British Columbia and territories	$64,185.41
Manitoba/Saskatchewan/Alberta	$59,519.62
Ontario	$62,352.18
Quebec	$58,021.52
Atlantic	$57,983.15

Highest Degree

In 2003 the difference between median salaries of speech-language pathologists with doctorate degrees and those with master's degrees was $10,114. Speech-language pathologists with doctorate degrees reported a median salary of $57,114, as compared to those with a master's degree who reported a median salary of $47,000. These median salaries were computed from combined academic and calendar year salaries.

Years of Experience

Salaries increase with the number of years' experience in the profession. For example, for a certified speech-language pathologist with one to three years of experience in 2003, the median salary for a calendar year was $42,000, as compared with the salary of $55,000 for a certified speech-language pathologist with ten to fifteen years of experience.

Other Benefits

When considering financial rewards, remember to include the value of the benefits package with the salary. Benefits packages such as insurance programs (medical, dental, disability, retirement) and leave (personal, sick, vacation) are available to speech-language pathologists in most employment settings. Their value, however, will vary depending upon the employer. Additionally, some employers provide ASHA dues, state association dues, licensure fees, and continuing-education fees. Many employers also provide financial support for external continuing-education programs.

Summary

Given the variety of employment settings and functions, speech-language pathologists find there are many personal rewards. The satisfaction that is derived from serving others is the reward that is cited consistently from persons who have enjoyed a productive and successful career in speech-language pathology. Additionally, depending upon the speech-language pathologist's education, credentials, years of experience, employment setting, and region of the country where employed, significant financial rewards are also attainable.

5

EDUCATIONAL PREPARATION

To PREPARE FOR a career in speech-language pathology requires a background in prescience/health, mathematics, and liberal arts, and a stalwart foundation in oral and written communication skills beginning at the high school level and continuing through graduate training. This chapter describes educational requirements in the United States and Canada including an identification of the areas of study typically required and degrees granted, description of admission requirements, description of programs in communication sciences and disorders, and identification of means of financial support that are available.

Educational Requirements in the United States

Following is a description of the educational levels and the areas of study and degrees granted for each. Requirements for admission to graduate study are also discussed.

High School

During high school, prospective speech-language pathologists should consider courses in biology, physics, social sciences, English, mathematics, language, psychology, and public speaking.

There is fierce competition to meet college entry requirements. Hence, students need to focus on maintaining at minimum a B average. Additionally, it is not too early to begin enhancing your reading and standardized test-taking skills. It is important to note that there is no particular high school emphasis required to enter this profession.

Undergraduate Training

Preprofessional course work can be completed either in an exclusively undergraduate institution or in a college or university in which graduate work in speech-language pathology can be taken. Since many other professions bear a direct relationship to speech-language pathology, a broad liberal arts education is recommended. Courses in biology, anatomy, psychology, human development, and anthropology can provide a valuable background. Special fields of study related to speech and language, such as linguistics, general semantics, and phonetics are also helpful.

A program of study in communication sciences and disorders is available at the undergraduate level. Courses in speech-language pathology are offered in these programs, and they provide a useful introduction to professional course work. Additionally, some of these undergraduate programs provide students with direct clinical practicum experience; that is, the student is supervised in direct clinical experience in the evaluation and/or management of clients with a variety of speech and language impairments. It is not, however, mandatory that students earn a bachelor's degree in communication sciences and disorders, although some graduate programs have this preference.

When you are ready to select an undergraduate program, look for one that will provide you with a broad educational experience in liberal arts. Remember, this should also include a strong foundation in oral and written communication. If you want to identify undergraduate programs that offer programs in communication sciences and disorders, send an e-mail to ASHA's Action Center at actioncenter@asha.org and request a copy of the list of U.S. programs in communication sciences and disorders.

While working on your undergraduate degree, seek opportunities to get an understanding of the profession beyond the classroom. Shadow several speech-language pathologists in various employment settings as they work with persons who have different communication disorders. This will give you an opportunity to experience a real workday and see if you like the pace, type of work, work environment, and professional colleagues.

Graduate Training

Although the curriculum of each college and university may vary from others, the following basic content areas are covered within all professional curricula.

- Fundamental studies of the processes of normal speech and hearing, including anatomy and physiology, acoustics, and the psychological aspects of human communication
- Nature and management of disorders of speech, language, and hearing

- Measurement and evaluation of speech production, language abilities, and auditory processes
- Management procedures, such as principles in remedial methods used in habilitation and rehabilitation of children and adults with various communication disorders
- Research methodology in the study of disorders of communication

To be more specific, courses necessary to provide fundamental information about normal development and use of speech and language may include the following: anatomy and physiology of the speech and hearing mechanisms, linguistics, physics of sound, phonetics, acoustic phonetics, speech science, psychology of language, language and speech acquisition, psycholinguistics, sociolinguistics, verbal learning, cognitive processes, and so forth.

Courses relevant to disorders of communication may include neurological communication disorders, language disorders, voice disorders, fluency disorders, articulation disorders, aphasia, aural rehabilitation, dysphagia, and so forth.

Examples of courses that supplement the management of communication disorders may include the psychology of personality adjustment, psychology and education of the exceptional child, psychometrics, psychology of learning, abnormal psychology, clinical psychology, counseling, interviewing, and social work.

Graduate degrees in communication sciences and disorders vary depending on the university. Some confer a master's in science, some a master's in the arts, others a master's in education. The type of degree may depend on the actual location of the program on the organizational chart of the university. Some speech-language pathologists pursue additional training beyond the master's degree. They obtain a doctoral degree: either a doctor of education (Ed.D.)

or a doctor of philosophy (Ph.D.). In some areas of practice, such as college/university teaching and administration, research, and private practice, a doctoral degree is desirable.

Admission Requirements

Admission into graduate programs in communication sciences and disorders has been very competitive over the past several years. In some instances more than three hundred students have applied for forty available slots. While each academic program has its own criteria for admission, most graduate programs like to see a grade point average of 3.4 or higher. Students who perform well in core courses such as science, mathematics, and the humanities are very attractive to the admissions committee. Additionally the majority of graduate programs require the Graduate Record Examination (GRE). You should contact the college or university that you are interested in to obtain information about the minimum GRE score required for its admissions. If you have not done well previously on standardized tests, then consider enrolling in a review course. Other admission requirements are likely to include a request for an official transcript, letters of recommendation, and an essay. Some programs have moved toward individual and group interviews.

Here are some tips to use when applying to a graduate program.

1. Visit the program's website and obtain a graduate school catalog to become familiar with the school's requirements and expectations.
2. Get in touch with the chairperson and let him or her know that you are interested in the program and plan to apply.
3. Visit the university and college campus. Meet with faculty, students, and alumni. The information you receive from an

on-site visit can help validate what you found on the website or in the printed materials describing the program. Here are some questions to consider asking while on your visit:

- What do you like most about this program?
- What do you like least?
- What kind of support do you receive from the faculty?
- How does your clinical experience prepare you for your career?
- What kind of clinical experiences do you have?
- Are there opportunities to network with practicing professionals?
- Is there an active student organization?
- Are students encouraged and supported to do research, make presentations, and attend conferences?
- Given what you know now, would you reenroll in this program? If yes, why? If no, why not?
- Would you recommend this program to a friend, colleague, student?

Make sure your application is complete and has no errors. Get someone to proofread it for you. Ask persons who have taught you more than one class to write letters of recommendation. If you have conducted research, engaged in volunteer work, or assumed a leadership position within an organization, get persons who can speak to these areas and your skills to write a letter of recommendation as well. If you did poorly in a previous course due to extenuating circumstances, include the reasons for your poor performance in your letter and speak to the reasons this grade is not indicative of your true academic abilities.

U.S. Programs in Communication Sciences and Disorders

To date there are more than three hundred undergraduate and graduate programs in the profession.

When selecting a graduate program, you want to make sure that it is accredited by the American Speech-Language-Hearing Association Council on Academic Accreditation. This accreditation ensures that the academic and clinical practicum experience meets the nationally established standards. Additionally, this accreditation is now necessary if you are to meet the requirements for the Certificate of Clinical Competence. A list of accredited programs is included in Appendix A.

For additional information about graduate programs, you can visit ASHA's online guide to graduate programs at www.asha.org, e-mail a request to academicaffairs@asha.org, or write directly to American Speech-Language-Hearing Association, 10801 Rockville Pike, Rockville, Maryland 20852.

If you are interested in a program with an emphasis in minority issues or a bilingual focus, the ASHA website (www.asha.org) contains a list of colleges and universities with such programs. A list of such programs as of 2004 can be found in Appendix B. You will need to contact these programs to verify that this specific emphasis continues to exist.

Educational Requirements in Canada

Professional training in speech-language pathology is available at the master's level at nine Canadian universities, three of which teach programs in French. (A list of these programs can be found in

Appendix C.) Canadian programs meet provincial licensure and the Canadian Association of Speech-Language Pathologists and Audiologists (CASLPA) certification requirements. Students who enroll in a program in the United States should ensure that the program meets the necessary licensure and certification requirements of Canada if they want to work in Canada.

While each graduate program has special requirements, the following undergraduate studies are required to enter at the master's level: courses in psychology, physiology, linguistics, education, human sciences, and health sciences. Graduate courses include acoustics, anatomy, assessment, counseling, hearing disorders, language development and disorders, linguistics, neurology and neurophysiology, nonvocal communication, parent training, psychology, phonetics, speech disorders, statistics, stuttering, voice and voice disorders, and a variety of specific areas (such as autism). The courses and clinical practica cover the development, disorders, and the training or retraining of human communication in all its aspects.

Considerations When Selecting a Program

When selecting either an undergraduate or graduate program, obtain information about several programs so that you can make comparisons. Create a checklist that identifies the characteristics of the program that you want to attend (for example, student/teacher ratio, program size, faculty area of expertise, clinical opportunities, distinguished alumni, and so forth), and then rate the programs based upon the material received. If possible, you may want to visit the programs and/or talk to alumni.

Financial Support for U.S. Programs

If you are enrolled in a program at least half-time or have been accepted for enrollment and are a citizen or permanent resident of the United States, you may be eligible for federal financial aid, loans, or scholarships. Given the competition for financial support, you should begin the application process at least three to six months in advance of the established time frames. A description of the available resources follows, and a list of financial aid options is also provided.

Federal Government Programs

The following programs are supported by the United States Department of Education:

Pell Grant Program for Undergraduate Students
Supplemental Educational Opportunity Grants (SEOG)
Supplemental Loans for Independent Students (NDSL)
Parents' Loan for Undergraduate Students (PLUS)
Guaranteed Student Loan (GSL) College Work Study
   Program

For information about these programs, order the free pamphlet *The Student Guide: Five Federal Financial Aid Programs*, from the U.S. Department of Education, Department DEA-87, Pueblo, Colorado 81009. You may also contact the U.S. Department of Education, Office of Student Financial Assistance, 400 Maryland Avenue SW, Room 4661, ROB-3, Washington, DC 20202.

Training Grants

Contact the departments of communication sciences and disorders at individual colleges and universities regarding training grants for speech-language pathology that they may have available. Funding may also be provided by federal government agencies such as the following:

U.S. Department of Education, Office of Special
   Education and Rehabilitation Services
U.S. Department of Health and Human Services, Office of
   Maternal and Child Health
The National Institutes of Health, National Institute on
   Deafness and Other Related Communication Disorders
American Speech-Language-Hearing Foundation
   Scholarships and Grants Program

Up to ten graduate student scholarships are available annually for master's or doctoral-level students studying audiology or speech-language pathology. Of the ten, one gives priority to a student with a disability, one gives priority to an international student studying in the United States, and one gives priority to a U.S. citizen who is a member of an ethnic or racial minority group. The scholarships range from $2,000 to $4,000.

Two $2,000 Student Research Grants are available annually to master's and doctoral students. One is for a one-year study in early childhood language development, and the other is for a one-year study in clinical rehabilitative audiology. For additional information, visit the foundation's website at www.ashfoundation.org or contact the ASHF at 10801 Rockville Pike, Rockville, Maryland 20852.

State Grant Programs

Contact special education departments, higher education assistance, and student or college aid commissions to learn about financial assistance available in your state. You may also contact the following organizations:

National Achievement Program for Outstanding African-American
   Students
One American Plaza
Evanston, IL 60201

National Hispanic Scholarship Fund
P.O. Box 748
San Francisco, CA 94101

National Merit Scholarship Program
One American Plaza
Evanston, IL 60201

National Scholarship Service and Fund for Negro Students
965 Martin Luther King Jr. Drive
Atlanta, GA 30314

Information about scholarships for Native American students seeking careers in health-care fields can be obtained from:

Indian Health Employees Scholarship Fund, Inc.
Executive Secretary
Federal Building, 115 Fourth Avenue SE
Aberdeen, SD 57401

The Sertoma International Scholarship Program is for students pursuing master's degrees in speech-language pathology programs accredited by the American Speech-Language-Hearing Association. Its address is:

Sertoma Foundation
Director, International Sponsorships
1912 East Meyer Boulevard
Kansas City, MO 64132

Universities

Most graduate programs have their own grant, scholarship, and loan programs as well as opportunities for part-time employment. You may inquire about these either through the graduate school or the communication sciences and disorders department.

Additional Resources

Funding Sources: A Guide for Future Audiologists, Speech-Language Pathologists, and Speech, Language and Hearing Scientists (Item #0112018), published by the American Speech-Language-Hearing Association, 10801 Rockville Pike, Rockville, Maryland 20852; or visit www.asha.org.

Need a Lift?, published annually by the American Legion, National Emblem Sales, P.O. Box 1050, Indianapolis, IN 48206.

Summary

Earning a master's degree is necessary if you plan to pursue a career in speech-language pathology. Meeting the academic and clinical practicum requirements are a must if you want the flexibility to practice in a variety of employment settings. If you wish to do research, teach at a college or university, or start your own practice, then you will need a doctoral degree. Given that a career in speech-language pathology will be one of the hottest in demand over the next decade, expect to compete for admission to graduate programs and for financial support. You must prepare, attend to details, and be conscientious and resilient—all characteristics of persons who have been successful in the career of speech-language pathology.

6

Credentials Needed
to Practice

To QUALIFY AS a speech-language pathologist, an individual must complete a comprehensive plan of study, both academic and practicum based, that culminates with either a master's or doctoral degree. The Certificate of Clinical Competence, licensure, and state certification are the credentials a speech-language pathologist needs to practice in different employment settings. In this chapter, for each credential the following is provided: an explanation of its importance, the organization or agency that is responsible for awarding it, requirements that must be met, and insights regarding the preparation needed to obtain these credentials. Additionally, the requirements that must be met to practice in Canada are identified.

Certificate of Clinical Competence

The Certificate of Clinical Competence (CCC) is the nationally recognized credential for speech-language pathology. That is, it is the only professional certificate that is recognized in every state. To practice in a variety of settings (clinics, hospitals, private practice), this credential is required. Additionally in most states, the eligibility requirements for licensure and certification are compatible with the CCC requirements. Therefore, persons who have been awarded the CCC more than likely can meet the requirements of other credentials needed to practice.

Who Awards It?

The American Speech-Language-Hearing Association (ASHA) issues the Certificate of Clinical Competence to individuals who present satisfactory evidence of their ability to provide independent clinical services to persons who have disorders of communication. Individuals who meet the standards as specified by the association's Council for Clinical Certification (CFCC) may be awarded a Certificate of Clinical Competence.

This CFCC, a semi-autonomous body, is charged with developing, interpreting, as well as applying the certification standards; formulating procedures for applications, examination, and review; awarding certification to qualified individuals; and through appointment of a special appeals panel, hearing and adjudicating appeals of certification decisions.

What Are the Benefits?

ASHA certificate holders will derive the following benefits from certification.

- They are able to provide or supervise individuals in the provision of clinical services.
- They are able to receive reimbursement from some third-party payers for services rendered.
- They have enhanced eligibility for promotion in some employment settings.
- They are ensured maximum flexibility in employment between states.
- They have an easier and more manageable state licensure process.

What Is Required?

The specific requirements include the following.

Degree

Applicants must have a master's or a doctoral degree. Effective January 1, 1994, all graduate course work and clinical practicum required must have been initiated and completed at an institution whose program was accredited by the Council on Academic Accreditation in Audiology and Speech-Language Pathology of the American Speech-Language-Hearing Association.

Course Work

Applicants must have earned at least seventy-five semester credit hours that reflect a well-integrated program of study dealing with: the biological/physical sciences and mathematics; the behavioral and/or social sciences, including normal aspects of human behavior and communication; and the nature, prevention, and evaluation and treatment of speech, language, hearing, and related disorders. Some course work must address issues pertaining to normal and abnormal human development and behavior across the life span and to culturally diverse populations.

(Note: One-quarter credit hour is equivalent to two-thirds of a semester credit hour.)

Basic Science Course Work

Applicants must earn at least twenty-seven semester credit hours in the basic sciences. At least six semester credit hours must be in biological/physical sciences and mathematics; six semester hours in behavioral and/or social sciences; and fifteen semester hours in basic human communication processes to include course work in each of the following three areas of speech, language and hearing—the anatomic and physiologic bases, the physical and psychological bases, and the linguistic and psycholinguistic aspects.

Professional Course Work

Applicants must earn at minimum thirty-six semester credit hours in professional course work. At least thirty of the thirty-six semester credit hours must be in professional course work in their major area of concentration (speech-language pathology). At least six semester credit hours of professional course work must be in the minor area of concentration (audiology). At least thirty semester hours of professional course work must be completed at the graduate level, and at least twenty-one of the thirty must be in the major area of concentration.

375 Hours of Supervised Clinical Observation/Practice

At least 25 hours of clinical observation must be completed, and 350 hours of supervised clinical practicum, of which 250 must be completed at the graduate level. The supervision must be provided by an individual who holds the Certificate of Clinical Competence in the appropriate area of practice.

National Examination in Speech-Language Pathology

Applicants must pass the examination. The current passing score is 600. This examination is designed to assess, in a comprehensive fashion, the applicant's mastery of knowledge of professional concepts and issues to which the applicant has been exposed throughout his or her professional education and clinical practicum. The applicant must pass the examination within two years of the date the course work and practicum submitted by the applicant is approved by the CFCC. An applicant who fails the examination may retake it. If the examination is not successfully passed within a two-year period, the applicant's certification file will be closed. The national examination is currently administered by the Educational Testing Service.

The Clinical Fellowship

After completing the academic course work and clinical practicum, the applicant then must successfully complete a clinical fellowship. The fellowship will consist of at least thirty-six weeks of full-time professional experience or its part-time equivalent. The fellowship must be completed under the supervision of an individual who holds the Certificate of Clinical Competence in speech-language pathology. The professional experience shall involve primarily clinical activities. During the clinical fellowship, the clinical fellow supervisor assesses the clinical fellow at least three times using the Clinical Fellowship Skills Inventory rating (CFSI). This form addresses the fellow's attainment of eighteen skills necessary for independent practice.

A person who holds the Certificate of Clinical Competence automatically subscribes to a Code of Ethics from the American Speech-Language-Hearing Association.

How Do I Prepare to Meet These Requirements?

Before selecting a graduate program, make sure that it is accredited by the Council on Academic Accreditation in Audiology and Speech-Language Pathology of the American Speech-Language-Hearing Association. Additionally, visit www.asha.org to ensure that the programs have maintained their accreditation.

Begin filling out the ASHA application while in the final semester of graduate school. Solicit assistance from your program director, including signing the application.

Sign up for a review course for the national examination. A number of institutions and associations have begun to sponsor preparation courses.

Meet with your potential clinical fellow supervisor. Make sure you understand how he or she plans to supervise and provide feedback to you. Communicate your expectations. It is important that you both understand each other's expectations prior to beginning your clinical fellow plan. You want this to be a meaningful experience, as well as one that meets the requirements for the CCC.

What Is Required to Maintain the Certificate of Clinical Competence?

All certificate holders must accumulate thirty instructional contact hours of professional development during each three-year certification maintenance interval to maintain their CCC. An instructional hour is sixty minutes that you spend in a professional development learning activity.

How Are Continued Professional Development Instructional Contact Hours Accumulated?

You can earn the necessary contact hours through one or more of the following options:

- Accumulation of thirty contact hours from employee-sponsored in-service
- Accumulation of thirty contact hours from other professional organizations' continuing education activities that contribute to professional development
- Accumulation of two semester hours (three quarter hours) from a college or university that holds regional accreditation or accreditation from an equivalent nationally recognized or governmental accreditation authority
- Accumulation of thirty contact hours (three CEUs) from a provider authorized by the International Association for Continuing Education and Training (IACET)
- Accumulation of three ASHA CEUs every three years

If you use ASHA CEUs, you will not have to keep records of your activities. Your ASHA CE Registry Transcript will be your verification of attendance. If you use instructional contact hours to maintain your CCC, you will be responsible for keeping records of your activities. For additional information about maintaining CCC requirements, visit www.asha.org.

Licensure

Licensure is a regulatory function of state government that allows individuals to practice after they have met specific requirements.

At present, forty-seven states require licensure in order to practice speech-language pathology. Consequently, in these states only those persons who meet the minimum requirements as defined in the state law can be licensed both to practice and to use the title "speech-language pathologist."

Three states (Colorado, Michigan, and South Dakota) and the District of Columbia do not regulate speech-language pathologists. Eleven states require school-based speech-language pathologists to be licensed (Connecticut, Delaware, Hawaii, Kansas, Indiana, Louisiana, Massachusetts, Montana, New Mexico, Ohio, Texas). Of the thirty-four states that officially regulate the use of support personnel, eleven states regulate through licensure (Idaho, Illinois, Kentucky, Louisiana, Maryland, Massachusetts, New Mexico, Ohio, Oregon, South Carolina, and Texas).

Who Regulates State Licensure?

Each state establishes a board to act as its licensing agency to prepare regulations, to implement the laws of that state, to review applications, to grant licenses, and to receive and adjudicate complaints against licensees. The board responsible for speech-language pathology licensure is most often referred to as the Board of Examiners in Speech-Language Pathology and Audiology and is usually comprised of speech-language pathologists. Some boards also include consumers and physicians as members. See Appendix D.

What Is Required?

The requirements for licensure vary from state to state. However, eligibility requirements in most states are compatible with the Certificate of Clinical Competence requirements. Additionally, many states will accept licensure from another state that has equivalent standards.

Continuing education activities have become a requirement in some states in order for licensure renewal. To date, forty-one states require continuing education. States vary also in the specifics for their continuing education requirements relative to time frame and content.

How Do I Prepare to Meet These Requirements?

Identify each state you are interested in. Contact the licensing board and request a copy of its requirements for licensure and application. To ensure you will meet the requirements, review your qualifications with your program director or a professional who is currently licensed in the particular state.

If the state where you will be working requires continuing education for licensure renewal, note the requirements. Develop an action plan that will ensure you meet them. You should review this plan periodically.

State Certification

This credential is required to practice speech-language pathology in the public school system. Therefore, if you are interested in working in this employment setting, you must meet the requirements for this credential.

Who Awards It?

Certification is issued by the state education agency. Appendix E provides a list of these.

What Requirements Must I Meet?

The requirements for certification vary from state to state, and they are not always consistent with the requirements for the Certificate of Clinical Competence. To date, twenty-nine states require a master's degree, eleven states require a bachelor's degree, and ten states require some other combinations.

How Do I Prepare to Meet These Requirements?

Identify each state you are interested in. Contact the state education agency and request a copy of its certification requirements to practice speech-language pathology. Review these with your program director or a person certified and currently working in the schools in the particular state.

What Is Specialty Recognition?

In 1995 the American Speech-Language-Hearing Association established a specialty recognition program. Speech-language pathologists who have advanced knowledge, skills, and expertise beyond the Certificate of Clinical Competence are recognized as specialists in a specific area of practice.

What Are the Benefits of Specialty Recognition?

Gaining specialty recognition can bring about personal satisfaction for being recognized by peers as a specialist in a specific area of practice. You can use this recognition to market yourself to clients, employers, and referral sources. Additionally, this recognition of advanced knowledge and skills can be used to negotiate higher salaries and reimbursement rates.

Who Awards Specialty Recognition?

The Specialty Recognition Program is operated by the Council for Clinical Specialty Recognition (CCSR) of the American Speech-Language-Hearing Association. This council established specialty boards, which are responsible for operating the specialty recognition program in the specific practice area.

What Are the Requirements?

This is a voluntary, nonexclusionary, and member-driven program. There are currently three practice areas that recognize specialists: child language, fluency, and swallowing and swallowing disorders. The requirements for specialty recognition vary. To obtain them contact the specific specialty board and visit www.asha.org.

Standards and Requirements for Practice in Canada

In Canada, the eligibility to practice is governed by provincial statute in the ten provinces. To ensure you meet the eligibility requirements for the province in which you expect to reside, it is necessary to contact the provincial association to determine its requirements.

The Canadian Association of Speech-Language Pathologists and Audiologists (CASLPA) grants professional certification on a national basis. The certification credential is voluntary, but it is recognized and accepted increasingly by employers and the public as a demonstration of professional competence. Certification is neither required by law to practice in any province nor required by Employment and Immigration, but individuals holding certification would likely meet the requirements for eligibility to practice in each province upon application and be viewed by the federal government as a qualified speech-language pathologist.

To be eligible for the CASLPA certification, a professional must:

- Possess a master's degree in speech-language pathology or its equivalent
- Hold full membership in CASLPA
- Pass the certification examination
- Meet practicum requirements

Is ASHA Certification Accepted by CASLPA?

As of January 1, 2005, ASHA has entered into an agreement with Canada that allows for the mutual recognition of certification in speech-language pathology.

What Is Needed to Maintain Certification?

Members must accrue forty-five continuing education equivalents (CEEs) over a three-year period. A wide variety of activities are acknowledged to reflect the interests of members and the opportunities available. Members must maintain records of their CEEs and submit a report annually in January to CASLPA. For additional information, contact the Canadian Association of Speech-Language Pathologists and Audiologists at 401-200 Elgin Street, Ottawa, Ontario, K2P 1L5, or visit www.caslpa.ca.

Summary

To practice in the employment setting of your choice, it is imperative that you meet the requirements for the credential necessary to practice in that setting. You will not be hired if you don't have the appropriate credential(s). Additionally, those persons seeking services from you and those referring clients will want to know that you are qualified. A minimum demonstration of being qualified is meeting the requirements for the credential to practice in your employment setting. Make sure you stay abreast of current requirements because credentials are essential to practice.

7

PREPARING FOR THE WORKPLACE

THIS CHAPTER DESCRIBES a process that can be followed to develop, nurture, and maintain a career in speech-language pathology. It involves defining career objectives, sourcing potential employment opportunities, developing a résumé, interviewing, following up, and the ongoing evaluation of career outcomes. Understanding and continuously improving this process is necessary to ensure a successful and productive career.

Defining Career Objectives

Once you have your degree in hand, what next? Oftentimes people just start searching for a job with no preconceived plan. A job may be found, but this does not necessarily lay the foundation for developing a career. To pursue a career and ultimately find the right job, prior to completing your training program you will need to begin to explore answers to the following important career questions.

• What populations do you enjoy working with the most? Think in terms of age and diagnosis.

• What feedback did you receive from your clinical supervisor(s), your clients, their family members/significant others, and referral sources?

• How did you feel at the conclusion of your clinical sessions and at discharge? Did you think you made a difference?

• What employment setting are you most comfortable working in? Think in terms of job expectations, opportunities for growth and development, compensation and benefits, fellow employees, and the culture of an organization.

• How much time do you want to spend engaged in various activities? Think in terms of direct service delivery, administrative duties, supervision, and meetings. Also, think about specific activities such as screening, conducting assessments, and intervening.

• Are there different job levels? Think in terms of clinician, supervisor, director, and so forth.

• Will you be encouraged and supported to attend continuing education programs?

• Will you be recognized for your contributions? Examine the incentives, rewards, and recognition program. Consider if these are consistent with the rewards that motivate you.

• Who will you work with? What is the culture like in this particular workplace? Make sure you meet the people you will be expected to work with, and then determine your compatibility. Consider the work tempo.

• What are your strengths and weaknesses? Think in terms of knowledge, skills, competencies, and personal attributes. In what areas have you demonstrated the most expertise? What areas have your instructors and supervisors identified that you need to improve?

• Are you flexible, open, persistent, organized, creative? Are these also requirements for the employer?

• Where do you want to be in the next three years? Do you want to provide services to a variety of clients? Do you want to focus in a specific area of practice? Do you want to work independently or with a team?

• What do you want to accomplish with your career and life? Do you want the quality of your clients' lives to have been improved as a result of your work? Do you want persons entering the profession better prepared because of your training? Do you want the delivery of services to have been enhanced because of a discovery you made? Do you want people to have access to services because you established a successful private practice?

You may find that you need to talk with your guidance counselor, advisor, instructors, supervisors, or even persons working in the profession to assist you in answering these questions. When you have answered them, write down your career objectives. You should be able to summarize them in single, concise sentences. Here are some examples:

• My objective is to provide services to the geriatric population that results in an improvement in their quality of life.
• My objective is to establish a profitable private practice that is recognized for the delivery of quality services.

Periodically it is important to review the career questions and your career objective(s). As you grow and increase your professional experiences, your career objectives will change. Therefore, these need to be reviewed, revised, and updated accordingly.

Sourcing Employment Opportunities

Where will you work? Before initiating a conversation with anyone about potential employment opportunities, you need to define a set of criteria that you will use to identify employment opportunities that will be appropriate for you. Below is a list of questions to get you started. You may think of additional ones to add to the list or you may decide some are not important to you and can be deleted.

Criteria for Identifying Potential Employment

Geography

- Do you want to work in the United States, Canada, or overseas?
- If you prefer the United States, what part of the country? South, Northeast, Midwest, Northwest, West? If you decide to work in Canada, then in what province?
- Do you want to live in a large city or a small town? Urban or rural area?
- Do you prefer a cold or warm climate?
- Do you mind commuting?

Employer Reputation

- Do you want to work in a setting that is respected by your professional colleagues and be recognized as a valid contributor to the community?
- Do you want your employer to have demonstrated that it has met professional standards and is accredited?
- Do you want an employer that is recognized as stable and has a track record of retaining employees?

Culture

- Do you want to work in an environment that continuously fosters open communication?
- Do you want to work in an environment that involves employees in decision making?
- Do you want to work in an environment that celebrates and recognizes employees' contributions?
- Do you want to work in an environment that facilitates and rewards teamwork?
- Do you want to work in an environment that fosters maintaining high standards and integrity?

Job Expectations

- How much time do you want to work in a given day or week?
- How much traveling are you willing to do?
- Are you willing to work on a team?
- How much documentation is required?
- How many meetings must you attend?
- How will you be supervised and evaluated?

Salary and Benefits

- What salary would you like? What is the lowest amount you will accept?
- What benefits do you want (insurance, retirement, vacation/sick leave, expense account, other perks)?

Growth and Development

- What promotion opportunities are there?
- How many job levels are there?

- What opportunities and support are there for continuing
  education?
- Are there any tuition reimbursement programs?

Define these criteria as best you can so that as you identify potential employers you will eliminate those that do not meet your expectations. It is always better to determine this prior to employment. Consequently, you may not have to change jobs due to unfulfilled expectations that can lead to dissatisfaction.

How can you find potential employment opportunities? There are several resources available to assist you in finding a potential employer. These include the following:

- **Personal contacts.** People such as instructors, alumni, friends, supervisors, and directors of programs where you have completed observations or a clinical practicum can usually give you the best leads.
- **Yellow pages.** These are located in the telephone book and provide a list of schools (private and public), hospitals, day-care centers, Veterans Administration facilities, nursing homes, and private practitioners.
- *ASHA Leader.* This American Speech-Language-Hearing Association publication is published twice monthly and contains classifieds listed by geographic location.
- **ASHA Online Career Center at www.asha.org.** This is an online center and resource you can use to search for job opportunities.
- **State education and regulatory agencies.** See Appendixes D and E.
- **Employment websites.** Go to www.hotjobs.com; www.mon ster.com; www.absolutelyhealthcare.com; www.jobs.nih.gov;

www.hospitallink.com; www.healthjobsusa.com;
www.carepathways.com; www.usphs.gov.

If you are a recent graduate, make sure that your potential employer will be able to provide supervision for your clinical fellowship year.

Developing a Résumé

A résumé is a brief account of your educational and professional experience. If it is effective, it will get you in the door of a potential employer, and it could lead to personal interviews that you might not otherwise have.

You can use your résumé for several different purposes: in response to an advertised position; as a "blind" inquiry about a job opening; attached to a standard job application; and to present during a job interview.

Your résumé should be detailed enough that a potential employer can assess easily your qualifications for a job opening. Below are some do's and don'ts that you should adhere to when you develop your résumé.

Dos

- **Be brief and to the point.** One page if possible; two pages maximum.
- **Forget rules about sentences.** Say what needs to be said in the fewest possible words; use phrases.
- **Stick to the facts.** Don't talk about your vacation, and so forth.
- **Use a spell-checker or have someone proofread the résumé.** Make sure there are no errors.

- **Make sure your résumé contains all the information that will sell you.** It may be as close as you will get to an employer.
- **Spend money for quality printing.** Make sure it is the best presentation you have ever made.
- **Organize your résumé in a clear-cut manner.** Key points should be easily recognized.
- **Use bullets, asterisks, or other symbols.** These will serve as "stop signs" that the reader's eye will be naturally drawn to. They will also make your résumé more navigable.

Don'ts

- **Don't be fancy.** Multicolored paper and all-italic type make résumés harder to read.
- **Don't ever send a résumé without a cover letter.** The cover letter should be directed to a specific person.
- **Don't allow typos.** Your résumé must be perfect.
- **Don't clutter your résumé.** Leave plenty of white space, especially around headings and margins.

The actual résumé-writing process involves the following steps:

1. Display prominently your name, address, home phone, and work phone.
2. State briefly your employment objective.
3. Provide information about your education and your certification, starting with your highest degree, the university from which it was awarded, and the date bestowed.
4. Explain your employment history. List each position, starting with your present one. Preface each description

with the title of your job. Capitalize the name of the position.

5. List any publications you have written or presentations you may have given.

6. List your honors and any special academic or nonacademic awards you have received.

7. List associations or societies to which you belong.

8. Include personal data, if desired.

The sample résumé and cover letter template in Figures 7.1 and 7.2 follow the format just described.

Interviewing

The interview provides you with an opportunity to get a close-up look at your potential employer. There are two critical questions that need to be answered at the conclusion of the interview: Are you right for the employer? Is the employer right for you? Remember, don't get so caught up in trying to demonstrate that "you are right for the employer" that you forget to determine if the "employer is right for you." Before the interview, be sure to find out:

- **Length of the interview.** How much time should you plan to schedule for the interview?
- **Interview format.** Will you meet with one person or several people individually, or will a team of people interview you?
- **Reimbursement policy/procedures.** If you are traveling from out of state, will the employer reimburse you for your expenses? What receipts must you maintain? When will you be reimbursed?
- **General information about the employer.** Make sure you know the basics: address of office you are visiting; headquarters

Figure 7.1 Sample Résumé

Jane Smith
1406 Lee Street
Orlando, Florida
407-555-1435

Employment Objective
Provide speech-language pathology services to the elderly in nursing facility or home.

Employment History
Clinical Fellow, 2005–Present, Jacksonville, Florida
Completed clinical fellowship year at General Hospital. Responsibilities included evaluating and treating adults with a variety of communication disorders including aphasia, dysarthria, apraxia, and dysphagia.

Speech-Language Pathology Trainee, 2003–5, Veteran's Affairs Medical Center, Washington, DC
Participated in grand rounds and care planning conferences. As a member of the dysphagia team, assisted in bedside and video-fluoroscopic examinations; participated in the decision-making process regarding patients' dietary needs; and provided direct treatment. Developed and implemented maintenance programs for patients with dementia.

Education
Master of Arts in Speech-Language Pathology, Michigan State University, East Lansing, Michigan, 2005
Bachelor of Science in Speech-Language Pathology, Hampton University, Hampton, Virginia, 2003

Honors
Dean's list for six semesters, graduated magna cum laude.

Associations
Florida Speech-Language-Hearing Association
American Speech-Language-Hearing Association

Figure 7.2 Cover Letter Template

(Your name)
(Your address)

(Date)

(Person's name)
(Title)
(Organization)
(Address)
(City, state, zip code)

Dear _____:

(First paragraph) Explain your reason for writing. Indicate the position about which you are inquiring. Tell how you heard about the opening or the organization.

(Second paragraph) Indicate one or two qualifications about yourself that would be of greatest interest to the employer. Tell why you are interested in the organization, location, or type of work. Mention any related experience or special training.

(Third paragraph) Make a specific request for an interview, indicating when you are available. Refer the employer to the enclosed résumé.

Sincerely,

(Your signature)
(Your name typed)

Enclosure

location, if different; relative size compared to similar employers' income and annual billings for the last two years; overall structure; major services, products, or research focus; history of the organization; names, titles, and backgrounds of top management; relative salaries as compared to those of similar employers; recent developments; and everything you can learn about the person(s) interviewing you.

Prepare a reference list of at least three persons. Include their titles, addresses, and phone numbers. Don't drop names. Make sure these are people who know your qualifications and can address them. Be prepared to give this list at the interview. Don't forget to tell your references that you will be submitting their names.

It will take a considerable amount of time to prepare for the interview, and prepare you must, if you want to stand out from the other candidates. The person who is well prepared and knowledgeable will be the most impressive.

The day of the interview, make sure you:

- **Wear conservative business attire.** Make sure your shoes are shined, nails cleaned, and hair cut and in place. Do not wear low-cut or tight-fitting clothes.
- **Arrive fifteen minutes early.** You will be able to get prepared for the interview, check your appearance, take a deep breath, check in with the receptionist, and get organized.
- **Shake hands firmly when you meet the interviewer.** First impressions are sometimes made based upon the handshake.
- **Maintain eye contact as you talk.** You want to demonstrate that you are confident and interested in what is being said.

- **Sit straight.** This is another means by which you communicate your confidence.
- **Accept something to drink only if the person conducting the interview will be drinking, too.** This could be perceived as a polite thing to do.

Remember that while on the interview, you are selling yourself. So it is vital that during the first five minutes you make a positive impression. How do you do this? By establishing rapport with the person interviewing you. This can be done through words, gestures, appearance, and common interests.

The interview process will vary, but you can anticipate an interview to follow this format: greetings; small talk; purpose of interview; general questions; specific questions; in-depth discussion about organization, job, and job opportunity; possible salary probe; and summary/next steps.

The majority of the interview will be questions and their answers—the interviewer's and yours. The following are examples of the types of questions you can expect on the interview. Also provided are suggestions regarding the type of questions you may ask. Additionally, a list of questions that are illegal is provided.

Interviewer Questions

What do you consider your greatest strengths and
    weaknesses?
In what setting would you feel most useful?
What could you contribute to this job? To the organization?
Why are you seeking a job with us?
In what area(s) do you think you need the most
    supervision?

What are your specific interests within speech-language
  pathology?

Have you had any experience dealing with personnel
  conflicts?

What are your future plans in the field?

How do you handle criticism?

How would you adapt your diagnostic/treatment style to
  our setting?

Do you see yourself as a supervisor?

Would you feel comfortable presenting an in-service to
  nursing?

Are you comfortable requesting orders from a physician?

How do you plan to achieve your career goals?

What two or three accomplishments have given you the
  most satisfaction?

Discuss a specific case that you found rewarding. What
  evaluations do you feel comfortable administering?

How do you feel about working with clients who seem to
  be making little progress?

How would you relate your intervention to the child's
  classroom work?

Tell me about the practicum experience you have had.

What language tests are you familiar with?

What has been your experience working with dysphagic
  patients?

How large a caseload could you handle?

What have you learned from your mistakes with patients?

For what reasons would you not treat a patient?

How much experience have you had dealing with parents
  and other family members?

What are your interests outside of work?

Tell me about your academic background.

What professional conferences or workshops have you attended?

At some future date, would you be willing to relocate?

How did you get along with your last supervisor?

Tell me about yourself.

What are your salary requirements?

Do you have any questions?

Preparing for the interview means not only having answers for the employer's questions, but also having a set of questions that you yourself would like to ask. Don't forget, when you leave you want to know "Is this employer right for me?" Below are examples of some questions.

Interviewee Questions

What will my typical day be like?

What happened to the last person who had this job?

Given my attitude and qualifications, how would you estimate my chances for career advancement in this organization?

Why did you decide to work here?

What do you like most about working here?

Given the chance, would you start here again?

How would you characterize the management philosophy of this organization?

What is this organization's long-range plan?

Does this organization have a vision, mission statement, basic beliefs?

What characteristics do the successful employees at this organization have in common?

How do you celebrate successes?

What's the best (and worst) thing about working here?

On the average, how long do employees stay here?

Who else can I talk to about the organization's culture?

Who determines my caseload size and composition?

What documentation is required?

What materials, equipment, and supplies exist? What can I order?

Who will be my immediate supervisor?

Is someone available to provide supervision for my clinical fellowship year?

Will I be supported to attend conventions, workshops, and other continuing education activities?

What kind of secretarial support is available? Will I have access to a computer?

Will my association dues be paid by the organization?

How will my job performance be evaluated?

There are some questions that the interviewer may not ask. These are more than inappropriate; they are illegal. According to the Civil Rights Act of 1964, organizations cannot discriminate in hiring on the basis of race, color, religion, sex, or national origin. Therefore, any questions in these areas are unacceptable. Additionally, there are other types of questions that should not be asked. These include:

- Any questions about marital status, number and ages of dependents, or marriage or childbearing plans

- Any questions about relatives, their addresses, or their place of origin
- Any questions about your arrest record. If security clearance is required, it is usually done after you are hired but before you start the job.

If the interviewer asks you some of these questions, first politely state that you don't understand how these questions pertain to the job. Ask the interviewer to clarify. If the interviewer persists, then you may need to bring up the legal issue. (If you get to this point in the interview, think about whether this is an organization you will enjoy working for.) Questions about possible discrimination should be referred to the Office of Compliance Programs, 2401 E Street NW, Washington, DC 20506, or to a district office. District offices are listed in the telephone directory.

Now that the questions have been asked, what next? Be sure to make a good last impression. Before the interview ends, summarize why you want the job, why you are qualified, and what in particular you can offer the organization. Ask for a business card so that you have the interviewer's correct title and spelling of his or her name for when you write your follow-up letter.

Following Up

It is important to get your impressions about the job and organization down on paper as soon as possible after the interview. Take out a sheet of paper and create two columns: "pros" and "cons." Indicate what you see as positive and list it under "pros." Then think about the negatives, the barriers, and list these under "cons." Look at both columns and decide whether this job is right for you.

Now it is time to write a thank-you letter (see Figure 7.3). Be sure it is typed. If you are still interested in the job, emphasize your reasons. Also, specify why you think you are the best person for the job. Indicate when you expect to hear from the interviewer. If you are no longer interested, thank the interviewer for taking the time to meet with you, and indicate that you are no longer interested in being considered for the position.

Regardless of your interest in the position after the interview, it is important that you send a thank-you letter immediately. This step is often overlooked in the job search process. However, it is very important and could prove to be a differentiating factor between you and your competition.

Ongoing Evaluation of Career Outcomes

To achieve your career objectives, it is important that you continue to assess your performance against them. Set a time frame for your self-evaluation. That is, will you review every six months? Annually? Biannually? Regardless of the time line, you should focus on two areas. These are:

1. **Given where I am today, what are my strengths and weaknesses?** After you have identified these, spend some time looking at those areas you consider weak. Now develop an action plan that focuses on improving them. Similarly, spend time looking at your strengths. Develop an action plan that identifies ways in which you will use these to assist you in accomplishing your objectives.

2. **Given where I am today, is this consistent with my objectives?** If not, why not? Identify barriers and opportunities. Look at the barriers and determine which you have control over. Now define

Figure 7.3 Post-Interview Thank-You Letter

(Your name)
(Your address)

(Date)

(Name)
(Title)
(Organization)
(Address city, state, zip code)

Dear _____:

(First paragraph) Express appreciation for the opportunity to be interviewed and refer to the position for which you were applying.

(Second paragraph) Indicate one or two areas discussed in the interview that were of particular interest to you. Mention your strong qualifications or background that will enable you to perform the job. Add any relevant experience that you omitted during the interview.

(Third paragraph) State that you would like the position and the reason you believe you would be an asset to the organization. Indicate that you are looking forward to the results of the interview and that you will call in a week to follow up.

Sincerely,

(Your signature)
(Your name typed)

steps to eliminate these barriers. Look also at the opportunities and define steps that will allow you to capitalize on these opportunities.

Summary

If you are to be successful in your pursuit of a career in speech-language pathology, it is imperative that you define your career objectives, pursue employment opportunities based upon these objectives, and continuously measure your performance against expectations. This ongoing self-evaluation will ensure that you stay on a path that will lead to a productive and rewarding career.

8

NETWORKING

THERE ARE A number of national and international professional networks available to speech-language pathologists. These networks provide a means by which you can stay abreast of current issues impacting the profession, share experiences with professional colleagues, learn from others, and identify professional opportunities. This chapter explains the importance of networking and identifies some networks that will be beneficial to you in your pursuit of a career in speech-language pathology.

Why Networking?

It is our human tendency to go it alone. But if you are to be successful, it is imperative that you network. There are two groups of people that you should target: those who can give you information about the profession and the industry, and those who are potential employers. Networking with these people will provide you with:

- **Information about the industry, profession, employers, and professional opportunities.** Knowledge and understanding of broad industry trends, financial health, hiring opportunities, and the competitive picture are essential if your career objectives are to be realistic and achievable. You would not want to wake up one morning only to learn that your job has been eliminated. This is possible if you have been isolated and are aware of only your immediate environment.

- **Information about hiring practices.** Knowledge about persons responsible for hiring decisions and hiring practices provides you with key information that will help facilitate your job search process. These persons and practices will change over time, so you need to stay current. As you pursue your career, you undoubtedly will also change jobs. Hence, at any given time, you want to know who to contact and what practices are acceptable.

- **Opportunities to sell yourself.** People will get to know you when you share with them your work and professional experiences, accomplishments, interests, publications, presentations, and research activities. A business card is a must. Every time you meet someone professionally, you want to give that person your card. This will make it easy for him or her to stay in contact with you. Naturally you would want professional contacts to remember you if an employment or professional opportunity that relates to your interests develops.

- **Opportunities to seek out advice.** You want to get input regarding professional issues and employment opportunities from the experts. It is important to identify persons who are knowledgeable about your professional interests. Also, you should identify key persons in leading organizations that employ speech-language pathologists. The information that they can share is invaluable and will assist you in making appropriate career decisions.

Make sure that you collect business cards from the persons you network with so that you can stay in touch with them. The relationships established while networking will prove to be as rewarding as the information exchanged and opportunities experienced. Having a support group will prove to be beneficial. And one day, you will be able to return the favor by assisting someone in his or her job search by providing information or making a referral. Networking is a reciprocal process. It never stops. The network is helped and so are you!

Whom Should I Network With?

You will find that the more contacts you make, the larger your job-related network grows. Here are two associations to get you started.

American Speech-Language-Hearing Association

The American Speech-Language-Hearing Association (ASHA) is the national professional, scientific, and credentialing association for speech-language pathologists, audiologists, and speech, language, and hearing scientists concerned with communication behavior and disorders. The association, a nonprofit organization, was founded in 1925. It has more than 120,000 members and affiliates in the United States and internationally.

The mission of ASHA is to promote the interests of and provide the highest quality services for professionals in audiology, speech-language pathology, and speech and hearing science, and to advocate for people with communication disabilities.

The American Speech-Language-Hearing Association maintains its permanent national office in Rockville, Maryland, where the executive, professional, and administrative staffs assist in coordinating the following association activities:

- Sponsoring national conferences, institutes, and workshops each year as part of its continuing professional education program
- Maintaining programs related to research, education, and delivery of clinical services
- Conducting an annual convention at which scientific sessions, exhibits, short courses, and other educational professional programs are offered
- Maintaining a national career information program, a governmental affairs program, and a public information program
- Carrying out a continuing program of data collection related to professional training, manpower needs, and membership characteristics and activities
- Sponsoring a voluntary continuing education program that approves providers of continuing education activities and offers an award for continuing education to certified individuals and members
- Publishing several professional journals and other professional materials
- Protecting the public interest by maintaining high standards for members, certificate holders, accredited clinics, and accredited programs

For additional information about the ASHA, visit www.asha.org or write to the American Speech-Language-Hearing Association, 10801 Rockville Pike, Rockville, Maryland 20852.

National Student Speech-Language-Hearing Association

This is the national organization for graduate and undergraduate students interested in the study of normal and disordered human communication that was founded in 1972. At present, there are more than eleven thousand students that hold memberships in chapters located on more than three hundred college and university campuses in the United States, Canada, Greece, Mexico, and Saudi Arabia. (Visit www.nsslha.org to obtain a list of current chapters.)

The National Student Speech-Language-Hearing Association (NSSLHA) is an association for students and managed by students. National policy and activities are governed by ten students (regional councilors) and five ASHA members (faculty). Students pursuing academic study as speech-language pathology assistants, students pursuing a doctorate of philosophy degree, and students enrolled in a communication sciences and disorders program outside the United States can be members of the NSSLHA.

Membership in the NSSLHA allows a student the opportunity to network with other students who are pursuing careers in speech-language pathology. The following are examples of some of the programs and activities sponsored by the NSSLHA to enhance the academic, preprofessional development, and networking experiences for students in communication sciences and disorders.

• **In the Loop.** This is an electronic announcement service that is a member benefit. Students receive monthly NSSLHA news and updates via e-mail.

- **Publications.** NSSLHA members will receive a newsletter, *NSSLHA Now!*, and a journal, *Contemporary Issues in Communication Sciences and Disorders* (CICSD). Both these publications are designed to provide the latest news and research impacting students in communication sciences and disorders.
- **NSSLHA member community.** This is an online member benefit that provides a place to exchange information and ideas. Members have an exclusive area to chat about the NSSLHA, chapter activities, conference and conventions, research, and "grab-bag" topics.
- **CICSD mentoring program.** This program is designed to assist students in publishing the results of their research. Students who have never published in a journal are eligible to participate.
- **NSSLHA Day at the ASHA convention.** Students can participate in events developed by the student leaders serving on the NSSLHA Executive Council.
- *Student Survival Guide.* This publication is designed to help students at any stage of interest in the profession learn what it takes to survive their academic study.
- **Advocacy program for students.** Students learn how to advocate for issues relevant to communication sciences and disorders and clients living with communication disorders.

Special Interest Divisions

Currently there are sixteen special interest divisions affiliated with the ASHA. These divisions are organized around a specific area of interest and are open to ASHA members, ASHA international affiliates, consumers, and students who are NSSLHA members. Each division also publishes a newsletter for its members, provides a members-only e-mail list, and offers discounts on selected short courses at the ASHA convention. Additionally, many are continuing education providers. The current list of special interest divisions includes:

Division 1: Language Learning and Education
Division 2: Neurophysiology and Neurogenic Speech and Language Disorders
Division 3: Voice and Voice Disorders
Division 4: Fluency and Fluency Disorders
Division 5: Speech Science and Orofacial Disorders
Division 6: Hearing and Hearing Disorders: Research and Diagnostics
Division 7: Aural Rehabilitation and Its Instrumentation
Division 8: Hearing Conservation and Occupational Audiology
Division 9: Hearing and Hearing Disorders in Childhood
Division 10: Issues in Higher Education
Division 11: Administration and Supervision
Division 12: Augmentative and Alternative Communication
Division 13: Swallowing and Swallowing Disorders (Dysphagia)
Division 14: Communication Disorders and Sciences in Culturally and Linguistically Diverse Populations
Division 15: Gerontology
Division 16: School-Based Issues

For additional information about each special interest division, visit www.asha.org.

State Associations

These are networks established at the state level. These associations provide members with an opportunity to identify resources and respond to issues at a local level. A list of state associations and addresses can be found in Appendix F. Other state networks that address specific issues include:

- **State education advocacy leaders.** The mission of this network is to enhance and perpetuate the advocacy, leadership, and clinical management skills of school-based ASHA members at the state and local levels to influence administrative and public policy decisions that affect the delivery of speech-language pathology and audiology services in school settings.
- **State reimbursement representatives.** These representatives are ASHA-member audiologists and speech-language pathologists who advocate locally with legislators, state insurance commissioners, health plans, unions, and employers on matters related to private health-plan reimbursement.
- **Medicare intermediary network.** This network is open to ASHA members only and focuses on enhancing and perpetuating the advocacy, leadership, and communication of ASHA members at the state level to influence administrative and public policy decisions that impact Medicare coverage, reimbursement, and delivery of speech-language pathology services and audiology services.
- **State licensing network.** Representatives of this network communicate actions and deliberations of state licensing boards for

speech-language pathology and audiology to promote a heightened awareness of licensing issues within their states; to share information with ASHA; and to ensure that the interests of both professionals and consumers are protected in state law and regulations.

For additional information about these and other networks, write to the American Speech-Language-Hearing Association, 10801 Rockville Pike, Rockville, Maryland 20852.

Canadian Association of Speech-Language Pathologists and Audiologists

This is the national voice for more than forty-six hundred speech-language pathologists and audiologists in Canada. The Canadian Association of Speech-Language Pathologists and Audiologists (CASLPA) was founded in 1964. It is the single national body that supports professional development and ongoing competency of speech-language pathologists and audiologists and champions the needs of people with communication disorders. CASLPA embraces members from all provinces and territories and ensures that they are represented in the association's board, committees, and task forces. Joining CASLPA provides you with numerous opportunities to collaborate with other professionals. An online directory is regularly updated, and the website features a chat room and members' forum. Additionally, CASLPA hosts events such as its annual conference that also facilitate networking.

CASLPA's staff is based in Ottawa and manages the association's publications, public relations and media awareness activities, governmental relations, and membership. Information regarding the association, membership, and networking opportunities can be obtained by visiting its website at www.caslpa.ca or by writing to the Canadian Association of Speech-Language Pathologists and Audiologists, 401-200 Elgin Street, Ottawa, Ontario K2P 1L5. Go to Appendix F for a list of Canadian Speech-Language-Hearing Associations.

International Association of Logopedics and Phoniatrics

The International Association of Logopedics and Phoniatrics (IALP) is a nonprofit, nonpolitical, and nongovernmental worldwide organization that works for the benefit of persons with speech, language, voice, swallowing, and hearing disorders. The organization was established in 1924 and has two major subfields: logopedics and phoniatrics. The IALP represents a professional body of 125,000 specialists in human communication through the fifty-six affiliated national societies from thirty-eight countries and more than three hundred individual members. IALP has informative status with UNESCO, UNICEF, and WHO and adopts the policy of nondiscrimination with respect to race, national origin, religion, handicapping conditions, and sex.

Persons professionally trained within the field of communication disorders and sciences may become individual members. National organizations of logopedics and phoniatrics may become affiliated members, category A. Multinational, regional, or local organizations pursuing wholly or partly parallel purposes may become affiliated members, category B.

Every three years the IALP holds an international congress to bring together members, associates, and other interested professionals from around the globe. These congresses are an opportunity to meet other professionals from different countries and cultures and to influence the development of communication disorders treatment on a global scale. The conference programs include presentations by internationally renowned speakers from all corners of the globe covering all aspects of speech, language, dysphagia, and hearing. The upcoming conferences are in Copenhagen, Denmark, in 2007; and Athens, Greece, in 2010.

For additional information about this organization, you can visit www.ialp.com.

Summary

There are many networks both national and international with which speech-language pathologists can affiliate. This affiliation is important throughout one's career. It provides an opportunity to meet and establish friendships that will be of support as you face career choices. Additionally, you will be aware of industry trends impacting the profession and can create opportunities, eliminate barriers, and be proactive versus reactive. Networking takes time, but it is worth the investment. The benefits will result in a more rewarding career.

9

The Future of the Profession

THE SCOPE OF practice for speech-language pathologists has changed over the past few years. Changes in federal mandates, more diverse clients, expanded use of technology, increasing demand for accountability, and shortage of speech-language pathologists all suggest the prospect for new opportunities and challenges in the near future. This chapter highlights some of the key factors that are fueling change and describes the perceived impact of these on the future of the profession.

Passage of Federal Laws and Regulations

Over the past ten years, there have been several federal laws and regulations passed addressing the needs of individuals with disabilities. These include:

Health Insurance Portability and Accountability Act
Individuals with Disability Education Act

Americans with Disabilities Act
Rehabilitation Act
Health Professions Act—Title VII of the Public Health
   Service Act
Disadvantaged Minority Health Improvement Act
Medicare and Medicaid

These federal mandates stipulate that all individuals (from birth to the elderly) with disabilities should have speech-language and hearing services when appropriate. Further, there are guidelines that ensure access to and payment for these services. Changes in these mandates will continue to have a significant impact upon the future of the profession, including productivity expectations, paperwork requirements, and the focus on outcomes data collection. Speech-language pathologists will continue to be challenged with doing and managing more with less. Additionally, there will be an increasing need for outcomes data to ensure reimbursement for services. Consequently, speech-language pathologists will need to be vigilant in the collection and reporting of data that demonstrate the quality and efficiency of service delivery.

Diverse Population

It is estimated that more than five million individuals from culturally and linguistically diverse backgrounds have a speech, language, or hearing disability. Cultural competence is recognized as an essential component of clinical competence. Speech-language pathologists will be challenged to develop culturally appropriate strategies for interacting with clients from cultures that are different from their own. The increase in diverse clients is also driving an increasing demand for bilingual speech-language pathologists and the sharing of information, ideas, concerns, and intervention approaches amongst professionals and clients across the globe.

Advances in Technology

The advent of the "computer boom" has fueled technological advances, including the development of artificial intelligence and expert systems. According to clinician Pamela Mathy-Laikko and professor David Yoder, other technological advances such as increased availability of digitized speech hardware and software, reduction in the size of microprocessors and peripherals, and expanded memory capacities are impacting the development of portable and versatile augmentative communication components.

Telepractice, the provision of services from one location to another using a telecommunications medium, proposes exciting promise to enhance the access and availability of speech-language and hearing services in remote areas and to persons who have transportation and mobility challenges. While the benefits are easily recognizable, there are issues that must be resolved to advance use of this methodology. These include finding innovative methods to facilitate connectivity (such as satellite technology, for example), making access to telepractice technology reasonable, maintaining confidentiality and privacy, and managing technology failures efficiently. Through telepractice, speech-language pathologists have the opportunity to create more effective intervention strategies.

Demand for Accountability

In this age of accountability and managed care, the future of the profession will in part be determined by the extent to which effectiveness of service delivery can be verified empirically. As such, an increasing emphasis is being placed on the importance of scientific evidence in guiding clinical decision making. The profession has begun to identify evidence-based practices. There is a need for future research to build upon this initial base. Speech-language pathologists will be challenged to use evidence-based research to produce better clinical outcomes and improve education and training programs.

Given these perceived changes and their impact, it is probably safe to suggest that we will continue to see changes in university and continuing-education training programs. These changes will impact both the focus and format of training, and the demand for continuing education will intensify. The continual changes in the profession will require that speech-language pathologists update their knowledge frequently.

To ensure continued advances in the profession, there will be a need for more clinical researchers. No longer will referral sources, payers, and consumers accept the "word" of the speech-language pathologist. Data will be essential. In fact, some form of reimbursement may be tied to demonstrated outcomes; payers will "pay for performance."

Summary

Speech-language pathologists will chart their new direction determined by the populations served, settings where they are employed, personnel utilized, technologies and procedures used, and data measured. The future promises to be challenging and full of many new opportunities. Although "tomorrow will not be like yesterday," one thing is for certain; the quality of many people's lives depends upon the manner in which speech-language pathologists take advantage of the opportunities that lie ahead and respond to these challenges.

Conclusion

If you are considering a career in speech-language pathology, to assist you in your decision making, identify several speech-language pathologists in the community, contact them, arrange to meet with them to discuss their practice of the profession, and schedule a time to shadow them so that you can experience a typical workday. Select persons who work with varied populations in different employment settings so that you can obtain the broadest perspective regarding what it is like to work as a speech-language pathologist. If, after spending time and experiencing a typical day with several speech-language pathologists, you find that a career in speech-language pathology is still of interest to you, then contact several accredited universities for information about their education programs. If possible, visit the universities and talk with students or graduates of these programs. For more career information contact the American Speech-Language-Hearing Association, 10801 Rockville Pike, Rockville, Maryland, 20852, or visit www.asha.org.

If you are interested in helping to make a difference in a fellow human's life, then speech-language pathology may be the career for you!

Appendix A

U.S. Graduate Programs in Communication Sciences and Disorders

THE INFORMATION PROVIDED here was obtained from the American Speech-Language-Hearing Association's Online Guide to Graduate Programs (1997–2005) at www.asha.org/gradguide. Unless otherwise noted, each school's master's program is accredited in speech-language pathology.

Alabama

Alabama A & M University
Department of Special
    Education
Speech-Language Pathology
    Program
P.O. Box 580
Normal, AL 35762
www.aamu.edu

Auburn University
Department of
    Communication Disorders
1199 Haley Center
Auburn University, AL 36849-
    5232
https://fp.auburn.edu/
    communication_disorders

University of Alabama
Department of
   Communicative Disorders
P.O. Box 870242
Tuscaloosa, AL 35487-0242
www.ua.edu

University of Montevallo
Department of
   Communication Science
   and Disorders
UM Station # 6720
Montevallo, AL 35115
www.montevallo.edu

University of South Alabama
Department of Speech
   Pathology and Audiology
Speech and Hearing Center
2000 University Commons
Mobile, AL 36688-0002
www.usouthal.edu/allied
   health/speechandhearing

Arizona

Arizona State University
Department of Speech and
   Hearing Science
P.O. Box 870102
Tempe, AZ 85287-0102
www.asu.edu/clas/shs

Northern Arizona University
Department of Rehabilitative
   Sciences
NAU Box 15045
Flagstaff, AZ 86011-5045
www.nau.edu/hp/dept/speech

University of Arizona
Department of Speech and
   Hearing Sciences
P.O. Box 210071
Tucson, AZ 85721-0071
http://slhs.arizona.edu

Arkansas

Arkansas State University
Program in Communication
   Disorders
P.O. Box 910
State University, AR 72467-
   0910
www.conhp.astate.edu/
   communicationdisorders

University of
  Arkansas–Fayetteville
Department of Rehabilitation,
  Human Resources, and
  Communication Disorders
Speech and Hearing Clinic
410 Arkansas Ave.
Fayetteville, AR 72701
www.uark.edu/depts/coehp/
  cdis.htm

University of Arkansas–Little
  Rock
Department of Audiology and
  Speech Pathology
2801 S. University Ave.
Little Rock, AR 72204-1099
www.uams.edu/chrp/audio
  speech/default.asp

University of Central
  Arkansas
Department of Speech-
  Language Pathology
201 Donaghey, Box 4985
Conway, AR 72035-0001
www.uca.edu/chas

California

California State
  University–Chico
Department of
  Communication Arts and
  Sciences/SPPA Program
First and Normal Sts.
Chico, CA 95929-0350
www.csuchico.edu/cmas

California State
  University–East Bay
  (formerly Hayward)
Department of
  Communicative Sciences
  and Disorders
25800 Carlos Bee Blvd.,
  MB 1099
Hayward, CA 94542-3065
http://class.csueastbay.edu/
  commsci

California State
  University–Fresno
Department of
  Communicative Sciences
  and Disorders
5048 N. Jackson Ave.,
  MS-80
Fresno, CA 93740-8022
www.csufresno.edu/csd

California State
   University–Fullerton
Human Communication
   Studies
800 N. State College Blvd.
Fullerton, CA 9283
http://communications
   .fullerton.edu

California State
   University–Long Beach
Department of
   Communicative Disorders
1250 Bellflower Blvd.
Long Beach, CA 90840-2501
www.csulb.edu/depts/
   comm-disorders/index.html

California State
   University–Los Angeles
Department of
   Communication Disorders
5151 State University Dr.
Kings Hall, B-106
Los Angeles, CA 90032
www.calstatela.edu

California State
   University–Northridge
Department of
   Communication Disorders
   and Sciences
18111 Nordhoff St.
Northridge, CA 91330-8279
http://hhd.csun.edu/comdis

California State
   University–Sacramento
Department of Speech
   Pathology and Audiology
6000 J St.
Sacramento, CA 95819-6071
www.csus.edu

Loma Linda University
Department of
   Speech-Language
   Pathology/Audiology
Nichol Hall
Loma Linda, CA 92350
www.llu.edu

San Diego State University
School of Speech, Language,
   and Hearing Sciences
5500 Campanile Dr.
San Diego, CA 92182-1518
http://slhs.sdsu.edu/index.php

San Francisco State University
Department of Special
  Education
Communicative Disorders
  Program
1600 Holloway Ave.
Burk Hall, Room 101
San Francisco, CA 94132-
  4158
www.sfsu.edu/~spedcd/
  programs/cd.htm

San Jose State University
Communicative Disorders and
  Sciences
1 Washington Sq. (SH 115)
San Jose, CA 95192-0079
www.sjsu.edu

University of the Pacific
Department of Speech-
  Language Pathology
3601 Pacific Ave.
Stockton, CA 95211
www.uop.edu

University of Redlands
Department of
  Communicative Disorders
1200 E. Colton Ave.
P.O. Box 3080
Redlands, CA 92373-0999
www.redlands.edu

Colorado

University of
  Colorado–Boulder
Department of Speech,
  Language, and Hearing
  Sciences
2501 Kittredge Loop Rd.
409 UCB
Boulder, CO 80309-0409
www.colorado.edu/slhs

University of Northern
  Colorado
Audiology and Speech-
  Language Sciences
Gunter 1400, Box 140
Greeley, CO 80639-0030
www.unco.edu/hhs

Connecticut

Southern Connecticut State
University
Department of
Communication Disorders
501 Crescent St.
Davis Hall
New Haven, CT 06515
www.southernct.edu

University of Connecticut
Department of
Communication Sciences
Unit 1085, 850 Bolton Rd.
Storrs, CT 06269-1085
http://speechlab.coms.uconn
.edu

District of Columbia

Gallaudet University
Department of Audiology and
Speech-Language
Pathology
800 Florida Ave. NE
Washington, DC 20002-3695
www.gallaudet.edu

George Washington
University
Department of Speech and
Hearing Science
2201 G St. NW
Room 424, Funger Hall
Washington, DC 20052
www.gwu.edu/~sphr

Howard University
Department of
Communication Sciences
and Disorders
525 Bryant St. NW
John H. Johnson Bldg.
Washington, DC 20059
www.howard.edu/school
communications/csd/
about.htm

University of the District of
Columbia
Department of Languages and
Communication Disorders
Speech-Language Pathology
Program
4200 Connecticut Ave. NW,
Bldg. 41, Rm. 413-0
Washington, DC 20008
www.udc.edu

Florida

Florida Atlantic University
Communication Sciences and
  Disorders
Communication Disorders
  Program
777 Glades Rd.
P.O. Box 3091
Boca Raton, FL 33431
www.coe.fau.edu/csd

Florida International
  University
Communication Sciences and
  Disorders
HLS 143–University Park
Miami, FL 33199
http://chua2.fiu.edu/csd

Florida State University
Department of
  Communication Disorders
107 RRC, Florida State
  University
Tallahassee, FL 32306-1200
www.comm.fsu.edu

Nova Southeastern University
  (Speech-Language
  Pathology)
Speech-Language and
  Communication Disorder
1750 NE 167th St.
North Miami Beach, FL
  33162-3017
www.fgse.nova.edu/slp

University of Central Florida
Department of
  Communicative Disorders
HPA-2, Ste. 101
P.O. Box 162215
Orlando, FL 32816-2215
www.cohpa.ucf.edu/comdis

University of Florida
Department of
  Communication Sciences
  and Disorders
P.O. Box 117420
336 Dauer Hall
Gainesville, FL 32611-7420
http://web.csd.ufl.edu

University of South Florida
Communication Sciences and
  Disorders
4202 E. Fowler Ave.
PCD 1017
Tampa, FL 33620-8150
www.usf.ed

Georgia

Armstrong Atlantic State
  University
Special Education/Speech-
  Language Pathology
  Program
11935 Albercorn St.
Savannah, GA 31419-1997
www.armstrong.edu

Georgia State University
Communication Disorders
  Program
MSC 6A0820
33 Gilmer St. SE, Unit 6
Atlanta, GA 30303-3086
http://education.gsu.edu/epse

University of Georgia
Department of
  Communication Sciences
  and Disorders
516 Aderhold Hall
Athens, GA 30602-7152
www.uga.edu

University of West Georgia
Special Education and Speech-
  Language Pathology
1600 Maple St.
Carrollton, GA 30118
http://coe.westga.edu/sedslp
Accreditation applicant in
  speech-language pathology
  (master's program)

Valdosta State University
Department of Special
  Education and
  Communication Disorders
Communication Disorders
  Program
1500 N. Patterson St.
Valdosta, GA 31698-0102
www.valdosta.edu

Hawaii

University of Hawaii–Manoa
Department of Speech
Pathology and Audiology
1410 Lower Campus Dr.
Honolulu, HI 96822-2313
http://manoa.hawaii.edu

Idaho

Idaho State University
Communication Sciences and
Disorders, and Education
of the Deaf
650 Memorial Dr., Bldg. 68
Campus Box 8116
Pocatello, ID 83209-8116
www.isu.edu/departments/
spchpath

Illinois

Eastern Illinois University
Department of
Communication Disorders
and Sciences
600 Lincoln Ave.
Charleston, IL 61920-3099
www.eiu.edu/~commdis

Governors State University
Program in Communication
Disorders
University Park, IL 60466
www.govst.edu

Illinois State University
Department of Speech
Pathology and Audiology
Mail Code 4720, 204
Fairchild Hall
Normal, IL 61790-4720
www.speechpathaud.ilstu.edu

Northern Illinois University
Department of
Communicative Disorders
DeKalb, IL 60115-2899
www.comd.niu.edu

Northwestern University
Department of
Communication Sciences
and Disorders
Frances Searle Bldg.
2240 Campus Dr.
Evanston, IL 60208-3540
www.communication
.northwestern.edu/cs

Rush University
Rush-Presbyterian-St. Luke's
  Medical Center/College of
  Health Sciences
Department of
  Communication Disorders
  and Sciences
1653 W. Congress Pkwy.
Chicago, IL 60612-3864
www.rushu.rush.edu/cds/
  communications.html

Saint Xavier University
Communicative Science and
  Disorders
3700 W. 103rd St.
Chicago, IL 60655
www.sxu.edu

Southern Illinois
  University–Carbondale
Communication Sciences and
  Disorders Program
1025 Lincoln Dr.,
  Rehn Hall #308
Carbondale, IL 62901-4609
http://web.coehs.siu.edu/
  publc/dgn_fin_frtyrd.asp

Southern Illinois
  University–Edwardsville
Department of Special
  Education and
  Communication Disorders
P.O. Box 1147
Edwardsville, IL 62026-1147
www.siue.edu/education/
  special_ed

University of Illinois at
  Urbana–Champaign
Department of Speech and
  Hearing Science
220 Speech and Hearing
  Science Bldg.
901 S. 6th St.
Champaign, IL 61820
www.shs.uiuc.edu

Western Illinois University
Department of
  Communication
Division of Communication
  Sciences and Disorders
121 Memorial Hall
Macomb, IL 61455-1390
www.wiu.edu/users/micom/
  wiu/csd/csd.htm

Indiana

Ball State University
Department of Speech
    Pathology and Audiology
AC 104
Muncie, IN 47306
www.bsu.edu/csh/spa

Indiana State University
Department of
    Communication Disorders
    and Special Education
8th and Sycamore St.
School of Education
Terre Haute, IN 47809
www.indstate.edu/coe/cd

Indiana University
Department of Speech and
    Hearing Sciences
Speech and Hearing Center
200 S. Jordan Ave.
Bloomington, IN 47405-7002
www.indiana.edu/~sphsdept/
    home.html

Purdue University
Department of Speech,
    Language, and Hearing
    Sciences
1353 Heavilon Hall
500 Oval Dr.
West Lafayette, IN 47907-
    2038
www.sla.purdue.edu/
    academic/aus

Iowa

University of Iowa
Department of Speech
    Pathology and Audiology
119 SHC
Iowa City, IA 52242-1012
www.shc.uiowa.edu

University of Northern Iowa
Department of
    Communicative Disorders
230 Communication Arts
    Center
Cedar Falls, IA 50614-0356
www.uni.edu/comdis

Kansas

Fort Hays State University
Department of
    Communication Disorders
600 Park St.
Hays, KS 67601
www.fhsu.edu

Kansas State University
Department of
    Communication Science
    and Disorders
303 Justin Hall
Manhattan, KS 66506-1403
www.ksu.edu/humec/fshs/
    fshs.htm

University of Kansas
Intercampus Program in
    Communicative Disorders
Department Speech,
    Language, Hearing
    Sciences and Disorders
3901 Rainbow Blvd.
Kansas City, KS 66160-7605
www.ku.edu/~splh/ipcd

Wichita State University
Department of
    Communication Sciences
    and Disorders
1845 Fairmount St.
Wichita, KS 67260-0075
www.wichita.edu/csd

Kentucky

Eastern Kentucky University
Department of Special
    Education
Communication Disorders
    Program
521 Lancaster Ave., 245
    Wallace Bldg.
Richmond, KY 40475-3102
www.eku.edu

Murray State University
Division of Communication
    Disorders
Graduate Program in Speech-
    Language Pathology
125 Alexander Hall
Murray, KY 42071-3340
www.murraystate.edu/
    academics/hshs/cdi/
    index.htm

University of Kentucky
Division of Communication
　Disorders
UK Charles T.
　Wethington Jr. Bldg.
900 S. Limestone, 124G
Lexington, KY 40536-0200
www.mc.uky.edu/
　commdisorders

University of Louisville
Surgery/Graduate Program in
　Communicative Disorders
Health Sciences Center, Myers
　Hall
University of Louisville
Louisville, KY 40292
www.louisville.edu/medschool/
　surgery/com-disorders

Western Kentucky University
Communication Disorders
1906 College Heights Blvd.,
　#41030
Bowling Green, KY 42101-
　1030
www.wku.edu

Louisiana

Louisiana State University and
　A & M College
Division of Communication
　Sciences and Disorders
64 Hatcher Hall
Baton Rouge, LA 70803-2606
www.lsu.edu

Louisiana State University
Health Sciences Center
Department of
　Communication Disorders
1900 Gravier St.
New Orleans, LA 70112
http://alliedhealth.lsuhsc.edu/
　communicationdisorders

Louisiana State University
Health Sciences Center in
　Shreveport
Department of Rehabilitation
　Sciences
Mollie E. Webb Speech and
　Hearing Center
3735 Blair Dr.
Shreveport, LA 71106
www.sh.lsuhsc.edu/ah

Louisiana Tech University
Department of Speech
P.O. Box 3165 T.S.
Ruston, LA 71272-0001
www.latech.edu

Southeastern Louisiana
   University
Department of
   Communication Sciences
   and Disorders
P.O. Box 10879-SLU
500 Western Ave.
Hammond, LA 70402
www.selu.edu

Southern University A & M
   College
Special Education/
   Communication Disorders
   Program
P.O. Box 11295
Baton Rouge, LA 70813
www.subr.edu

University of
   Louisiana–Lafayette
Department of
   Communicative Disorders
P.O. Box 43170
Lafayette, LA 70504-4170
www.louisiana.edu

University of Louisiana
Department of
   Communicative Disorders
700 University Ave.
Monroe, LA 71209-0321
www.ulm.edu/codi

Maine

University of Maine–Orono
Department of
   Communication Sciences
   and Disorders
5724 Dunn Hall
Orono, ME 04469-5724
www.umaine.edu/comscidis

Maryland

Loyola College in Maryland
Department of Speech-
   Language Pathology
4501 N. Charles St.
Baltimore, MD 21210
www.loyola.edu/clinics/
   index.html

Towson University
Department of Audiology,
  Speech-Language
  Pathology, and Deaf
  Studies
8000 York Rd.
Towson, MD 21252-0001
www.towson.edu/asld

University of
  Maryland–College Park
Department of Hearing and
  Speech Sciences
0100 Lefrak Hall
College Park, MD 20742
www.bsos.umd.edu/hesp

Massachusetts

Boston University
Programs in Communication
  Disorders
Department of Health
  Sciences
635 Commonwealth Ave.
Boston, MA 02215
www.bu.edu/sargent

Emerson College
Department of
  Communication Sciences
  and Disorders
120 Boylston St.
Boston, MA 02116-4624
www.emerson.edu/
  communication_disorders

MGH Institute of Health
  Professions
Graduate Program in
  Communication Sciences
  and Disorders
36 1st Ave.
Charlestown Navy Yard
Boston, MA 02129
www.mghihp.edu

Northeastern University
Department of Speech-
  Language Pathology and
  Audiology
360 Huntington Ave.
106 Forsyth Bldg.
Boston, MA 02115
www.slpa.neu.edu

University of
Massachusetts–Amherst
Department of
Communication Disorders
715 N. Pleasant St.
Amherst, MA 01003-9304
www.umass.edu/sphhs/comdis

Worcester State College
Department of
Communication Sciences
and Disorders
486 Chandler St.
Worcester, MA 01602-2597
www.worcester.edu

Michigan

Central Michigan University
Department of
Communication Disorders
441 Moore Hall
Mt. Pleasant, MI 48859
www.chp.cmich.edu/cdo

Eastern Michigan University
Special Education
Department/Program in
Speech-Language Impaired
110 Porter Bldg.
Ypsilanti, MI 48197
www.emich.edu/coe/speced/
gradprog.html

Michigan State University
Department of Audiology and
Speech Sciences
101 Oyer Speech and Hearing
East Lansing, MI 48824-1220
www.asc.msu.edu

Wayne State University
Department of Audiology and
Speech-Language
Pathology
581 Manoogian Hall
Detroit, MI 48202
http://sun.science.wayne.edu/
~aslp

Western Michigan University
Department of Speech
Pathology and Audiology
Kalamazoo, MI 49008-5355
www.wmich.edu/hhs/sppa

Minnesota

Minnesota State
University–Mankato
Communication Disorders
Program
103 Armstrong Hall
Mankato, MN 56001
www.mnsu.edu

Minnesota State
   University–Moorhead
Department of
Speech/Language/Hearing
   Sciences
1104 7th Ave. South
Moorhead, MN 56563
www.mnstate.edu/slhs

Saint Cloud State University
Department of
   Communication Disorders
720 4th Ave. South
EB A216
St. Cloud, MN 56301-4498
www.stcloudstate.edu

University of Minnesota
Speech-Language-Hearing
   Sciences
164 Pillsbury Dr. SE
115 Shevlin Hall
Minneapolis, MN 55455
www.slhs.umn.edu

University of
   Minnesota–Duluth
Communication Disorders
   Program
1207 Ordean Court
221 Bohannon Hall
Duluth, MN 55812-9989
www.d.umn.edu/csd

Mississippi

Jackson State University
Department of
   Communicative Disorders
3825 Ridgewood Rd., Box 23
Jackson, MS 39211-6453
www.jsums.edu

Mississippi University for
   Women
Speech-Language Pathology
1100 College St.
MUW-1340
Columbus, MS 39701-5800
www.muw.edu/speech

University of Mississippi
Department of
   Communicative Disorders
P.O. Box 1848
University, MS 38677
www.olemiss.edu/depts/
   comm_disorders/index.htm

University of Southern
   Mississippi
Department of Speech and
   Hearing Sciences
P.O. Box 5092
Hattiesburg, MS 39406-5092
www.usm.edu/shs

Missouri

Central Missouri State
  University
Department of
  Communication Disorders
Martin Bldg. 34
Warrensburg, MO 64093
www.cmsu.edu

Fontbonne University
Department of
  Communication Disorders
  and Deaf Education
6800 Wydown Blvd.
St. Louis, MO 63105-3098
www.fontbonne.edu

Missouri State University
Department of
  Communication Sciences
  and Disorders
901 S. National Ave.
Springfield, MO 65804-0095
www.missouristate.edu/csd

Rockhurst University
Communication Sciences and
  Disorders
1100 Rockhurst Rd.
Kansas City, MO 64110
www.rockhurst.edu

Saint Louis University
Department of
  Communication Sciences
  and Disorders
3750 Lindell Blvd.
McGannon Hall, Ste. 23
St. Louis, MO 63108
www.slu.edu/colleges/cops/cd

Southeast Missouri State
  University
Department of
  Communication Disorders
1 University Plaza
Cape Girardeau, MO 63701
www5.semo.edu/
  commdisorders

Truman State University
Department of
  Communication Disorders
Barnett Hall 222
Kirksville, MO 63501-4221
www2.truman.edu/comdis

University of
  Missouri–Columbia
Department of
  Communication Science
  and Disorders
303 Lewis Hall
Columbia, MO 65211
www.umshp.org/csd

Nebraska

University of
   Nebraska–Kearney
Communication Disorders
   Program
Welch Hall UNK
Kearney, NE 68849-4597
www.unk.edu/acad/cdis/home
   .html

University of
   Nebraska–Lincoln
Department of Special
   Education and
   Communication Disorders
301 Barkley Center
MABL 233
Lincoln, NE 68583-0234
www.unl.edu/barkley/index
   .shtml

University of
   Nebraska–Omaha
Special Education and
   Communication Disorders
6001 Dodge St.
Omaha, NE 68182-0054
www.unomaha.edu

Nevada

University of Nevada–Reno
Department of Speech
   Pathology and Audiology
School of Medicine
Redfield Bldg./152
Reno, NV 89557-0046
www.unr.edu/spa

New Hampshire

University of New Hampshire
Department of
   Communication Sciences
   and Disorders
4 Library Way, Hewitt Hall
Durham, NH 03824
www.unh.edu/
   communication-disorders

New Jersey

The College of New Jersey
Special Education, Language,
   and Literacy
2000 Pennington Rd.
P.O. Box 7718
Ewing, NJ 08628-0718
www.tcnj.edu

Kean University
Department of
Communication Disorders
and Deafness
1000 Morris Ave.
Union, NJ 07083
www.kean.edu/~keangrad/
grad_CE_slp.htm

Montclair State University
Department of
Communication Sciences
and Disorders
1 Normal Ave., Speech Bldg.
Montclair, NJ 07043
http://chss.montclair.edu/csd

Seton Hall University
School of Graduate Medical
Education
Department of Speech-
Language Pathology and
Audiology
400 S. Orange Ave.
South Orange, NJ 07079-
2689
www.shu.edu

William Paterson University
Department of
Communication Disorders
300 Pompton Rd.
Wayne, NJ 07470
www.wpunj.edu/cos/
comm-disorders

New Mexico

Eastern New Mexico
University
Department of
Communicative Disorders
Station #3
Portales, NM 88130
www.enmu.edu

New Mexico State University
Department of Special
Education/Communication
Disorders
SPED/CD New Mexico State
University
P.O. Box 30001/MSC3SPE
Las Cruces, NM 88003
www.nmsu.edu

University of New Mexico
Department of Speech and
  Hearing Sciences
1712 Lomas Blvd. NE
MSC01 1195
Albuquerque, NM 87131
www.unm.edu

New York

Adelphi University
Communication Sciences and
  Disorders
Hy Weinberg Center,
  Rm. 001
158 Cambridge Ave.
Garden City, NY 11530
www.adelphi.edu

Brooklyn College of CUNY
Speech-Language Pathology
  and Audiology
2900 Bedford Ave.
Brooklyn, NY 11210
www.brooklyn.cuny.edu

Buffalo State College
Department of Speech-
  Language Pathology
1300 Elmwood Ave.
Buffalo, NY 14222-1095
www.buffalostate.edu

College of Saint Rose
Communication Disorders
  Department
432 Western Ave., Box 100
Albany, NY 12203-1490
www.strose.edu

Hofstra University
Department of Speech-
  Language-Hearing Sciences
110 Hofstra University
DAV #106
Hempstead, NY 11549
www.hofstra.edu

Hunter College of CUNY
Communication Sciences
  Program
School of Health Sciences
425 E. 25th St.
New York, NY 10010-2590
www.hunter.cuny.edu/
  schoolhp/comsc/index.htm

Ithaca College
Department of Speech-
  Language Pathology and
  Audiology
953 Danby Rd.
Ithaca, NY 14850-7185
www.ithaca.edu/hshp/slpa

Lehman College of CUNY
Department of Speech-
Language-Hearing Sciences
250 Bedford Park Blvd. West
Bronx, NY 10468-1589
www.cuny.edu

Long Island
University–Brooklyn
Department of
Communication Sciences
and Disorders
1 University Plaza
Brooklyn, NY 11201-8423
www.brooklyn.liu.edu

Long Island University–C. W.
Post Center
Communication Sciences and
Disorders
720 Northern Blvd.
Brookville, NY 11548-1300
www.cwpost.liunet.edu

Mercy College
Communication Disorders
555 Broadway, Rm. 209
Dobbs Ferry, NY 10522
www.mercy.edu

Nazareth College of Rochester
Department of
Communication Sciences
and Disorders/Speech-
Language Pathology
4245 East Ave.
Rochester, NY 14618-3790
www.naz.edu

New York Medical College
Speech-Language Pathology
School of Public Health
Valhalla, NY 10595
www.nymc.edu

New York University
Department of Speech-
Language Pathology and
Audiology
719 Broadway, Ste. 200
New York, NY 10003
www.nyu.edu/education/
speech

Plattsburgh State University of
New York
Department of
Communication Disorders
and Sciences
101 Broad St.
224 Sibley Hall
Plattsburgh, NY 12901
www.plattsburgh.edu/cds

Queens College of CUNY
Department of Linguistics and
Communication Disorders
65-30 Kissena Blvd.
Flushing, NY 11367
www.qc.edu/lcd

Saint John's University
Graduate Program in Speech-
Language Pathology and
Audiology
8000 Utopia Pkwy.
Jamaica, NY 11439
http://new.stjohns.edu

State University of New
York–Buffalo
Department of
Communicative Disorders
and Sciences
3435 Main St., 122 Cary Hall
Buffalo, NY 14214-3005
http://wings.buffalo.edu/
soc-sci/cds/index.htm

State University of New
York–Fredonia
Department of Speech
Pathology and Audiology
W123 Thompson Hall
Fredonia, NY 14063
www.fredonia.edu

State University of New
York–Geneseo
Department of
Communicative Disorders
and Sciences
1 College Circle, 218 Sturgis
Hall
Geneseo, NY 14454
www.geneseo.edu/~cds/
cdsparts/cds_grad_program
.html

State University of New
York–New Paltz
Department of
Communication Disorders
75 S. Manheim Blvd., Ste. 6
HUM 14A
New Paltz, NY 12561-2499
www.newpaltz.edu

Syracuse University
Department of
Communication Sciences
and Disorders
805 S. Crouse Ave.
Syracuse, NY 13244-2280
http://thecollege.syr.edu/
depts/csd

Teachers College–Columbia
University
Speech and Language
Pathology and Audiology
525 W. 125th St.
New York, NY 10027-6696
www.tc.columbia.edu

Touro College
Graduate Program in Speech-
Language Pathology
1610 E. 19th St.
Brooklyn, NY 11229
www.touro.edu/gsp

North Carolina

Appalachian State University
Department of Language,
Reading, and
Exceptionalities
124 Edwin Duncan Hall, Box
32085
Boone, NC 28608-2085
www.lre.appstate.edu/
gr-cd/1gr-intro.html

East Carolina University
Department of
Communication Sciences
and Disorders
Greenville, NC 27858-4353
www.ecu.edu/csd

North Carolina Central
University
Department of
Communication Disorders
712 Cecil St.
Durham, NC 27707
www.nccu.edu/soe/depart
ments/communications/
communication_index.htm

University of North
Carolina–Chapel Hill
Division of Speech and
Hearing Sciences
CB# 7190, Wing D, Medical
School
Chapel Hill, NC 27599-7190
www.med.unc.edu/ahs/sphs

University of North
Carolina–Greensboro
Communication Sciences and
Disorders
300 Ferguson Bldg.
UNCG–Box 26170
Greensboro, NC 27402-6170
www.uncg.edu/csd

Western Carolina University
Human Services/
  Communication Sciences
  and Disorders
G30 McKee Bldg.
Cullowhee, NC 28723-9043
www.ceap.wcu.edu/commdis/
  cd.html

North Dakota

Minot State University
Department of
  Communication Disorders
  and Special Education
500 University Ave. West
Minot, ND 58707
www.minotstateu.edu

University of North Dakota
Department of
  Communication Sciences
  and Disorders
P.O. Box 8040
Grand Forks, ND 58202-
  8040
www.und.edu

Ohio

Bowling Green State
  University
Department of
  Communication Disorders
200 Health Center
Bowling Green, OH 43403
www.bgsu.edu/departments/
  cdis

Case Western Reserve
  University
Department of
  Communication Sciences
11206 Euclid Ave.
Cleveland, OH 44106-7154
www.case.edu/artsci/cosi/
  index.html

Cleveland State University
Department of Speech and
  Hearing
2121 Euclid Ave., MC 430
Cleveland, OH 44115
www.csuohio.edu/speech

Kent State University
School of Speech Pathology
  and Audiology
A104 Music and Speech Bldg.
Kent, OH 44242
www.kent.edu

Miami University
Department of Speech
 Pathology and Audiology
2 Bachelor Hall
Oxford, OH 45056-3414
http://casnov1.cas.muohio
 .edu/spa

Ohio State University
Department of Speech and
 Hearing Sciences
110 Pressey Hall
1070 Carmack Rd.
Columbus, OH 43210-1002
www.osu.edu/sphs

Ohio University
School of Hearing, Speech,
 and Language Sciences
Grover Center W218
Athens, OH 45701-2979
www.ohiou.edu/hearingspeech

University of Akron
School of Speech-Language
 Pathology and Audiology
Polsky Bldg., Rm. 181
Akron, OH 44325-3001
www.uakron.edu/sslpa

University of Cincinnati
Communication Sciences and
 Disorders
Mail Location 379
Cincinnati, OH 45267-0379
www.uc.edu/csd

University of Toledo
Public Health and
 Rehabilitative Services
2801 W. Bancroft St.
Toledo, OH 43606
www.utoledo.edu

Oklahoma

Northeastern State University
Department of Health
 Professions
Speech-Language Pathology
 Program
Special Services Bldg., NSU
600 N. Grand
Tahlequah, OK 74464-7051
www.nsuok.edu

Oklahoma State University
Department of
 Communication Sciences
 and Disorders
110 Hanner Bldg.
Stillwater, OK 74078-5062
www.okstate.edu

University of Central
   Oklahoma
Special Services–Speech-
   Language Pathology
   Program
100 N. University Dr.
Edmond, OK 73034
www.educ.ucok.edu/sps/
   graduate.asp#speech

University of Oklahoma
Health Sciences Center
Department of
   Communication Sciences
   and Disorders
825 NE 14th St.
P.O. Box 26901
Oklahoma City, OK 73910
www.ouhsc.edu

University of Tulsa
Department of
   Communication Disorders
600 S. College Ave.
Tulsa, OK 74104-3189
www.utulsa.edu/graduate

Oregon

Portland State University
Speech and Hearing Sciences
   Program
P.O. Box 751
Portland, OR 97207-0751
www.sphr.pdx.edu

University of Oregon
Communication Disorders
   and Sciences Program
5284 University of Oregon
Eugene, OR 97403-5284
http://education.uoregon.edu/
   field.htm?id=45

Pennsylvania

Bloomsburg University
Department of Audiology and
   Speech Pathology
400 E. 2nd St., Centennial
   Hall
Bloomsburg, PA 17815-1301
www.bloomu.edu

California University of
Pennsylvania
Department of
Communication Disorders
250 University Ave.
California, PA 15419
www.cup.edu

Clarion University of
Pennsylvania
Department of
Communication Sciences
and Disorders
840 Wood St.
118 Keeling Health Center
Clarion, PA 16214-1232
www.clarion.edu

College Misericordia
Department of Speech-
Language Pathology
McAuley Hall, Rm. 305
301 Lake St.
Dallas, PA 18612
www.misericordia.edu/academ
ics/healthweb/speech
language/index.htm
(Accreditation candidate in
speech-language
pathology—master's
program)

Duquesne University
Department of Speech-
Language Pathology
600 Forbes Ave.
Pittsburgh, PA 15282
www.duq.edu

East Stroudsburg University of
Pennsylvania
Speech Pathology and
Audiology
LaRue Hall
East Stroudsburg, PA 18301-
2999
www.esu.edu

Edinboro University of
Pennsylvania
Speech and Communication
Studies/Speech-Language
Pathology
115A Compton Hall
Edinboro, PA 16444
www.edinboro.edu

Indiana University of
Pennsylvania
Special Education and Clinical
Services
Speech-Language Pathology
Program
203 Davis Hall
570 S. 11th St.
Indiana, PA 15705
www.coe.iup.edu/special-ed/
slp.htm

La Salle University
Speech-Language-Hearing
Sciences Program
1900 W. Olney Ave.
Philadelphia, PA 19141
www.lasalle.edu/speech

Marywood University
Department of
Communication Sciences
and Disorders
McGowan Center
2300 Adams Ave.
Scranton, PA 18509-1598
www.marywood.edu

Pennsylvania State University
Department of
Communication Sciences
and Disorders
110 Moore Bldg.
University Park, PA 16802-
3100
http://csd.hhdev.psu.edu

Temple University
Communication Sciences
1701 N. 13th St.
110 Weiss Hall
Philadelphia, PA 19122
www.temple.edu/commsci

University of Pittsburgh
Communication Science and
Disorders
4033 Forbes Tower,
Atwood St.
Pittsburgh, PA 15260
www.shrs.pitt.edu/csd

West Chester University
Department of
Communicative Disorders
201 Carter Dr.
West Chester, PA 19383
www.wcupa.edu

Puerto Rico

University of Puerto Rico
Department of Graduate
Programs, Speech-
Language Pathology
Program and Audiology
P.O. Box 365067
San Juan, PR 00936-5067
www.rcm.upr.edu

Rhode Island

University of Rhode Island
Department of
Communicative Disorders
Independence Sq., Ste. 1
25 W. Independence Way
Kingston, RI 02881-0821
www.uri.edu/hss/cmd

South Carolina

Medical University of South
Carolina
Communication Sciences and
Disorders Program
77 President St., Ste. 117
Charleston, SC 29425
www.musc.edu/csd

South Carolina State
University
Department of Speech
Pathology and Audiology
P.O. Box 7427
300 College St. NE
Orangeburg, SC 29117
www.scsu.edu

University of South Carolina
Department of
Communication Sciences
and Disorders
Columbia, SC 29208
www.sph.sc.edu

South Dakota

University of South Dakota
Department of
Communication Disorders
414 E. Clark St.
Vermillion, SD 57069-2390
www.usd.edu/dcom

Tennessee

East Tennessee State
University
Department of
Communicative Disorders
P.O. Box 70643
Johnson City, TN 37614
www.etsu.edu/cpah/commdis

Tennessee State University
Department of Speech
Pathology and Audiology
330 10th Ave. North, Ste. A
Box 131
Nashville, TN 37203-3401
www.tnstate.edu

University of Memphis
School of Audiology and
Speech-Language
Pathology
807 Jefferson Ave.
Memphis, TN 38105
www.ausp.memphis.edu

University of
Tennessee–Knoxville
Department of Audiology and
Speech Pathology
576 S. Stadium Hall
Knoxville, TN 37996
http://web.utk.edu/~aspweb

Vanderbilt University
Division of Hearing and
Speech Sciences
1114 19th Ave. South
Nashville, TN 37212
http://vanderbiltbillwilkerson
center.com/dhss.html

Texas

Abilene Christian University
Communication Sciences and
Disorders Division
ACU Box 28058
Abilene, TX 79699-8058
www.acu.edu

Baylor University
Department of
Communication Sciences
and Disorders
1 Bear Pl., #97332
Waco, TX 76798-7056
www.baylor.edu

Lamar University–Beaumont
Department of
Communication Disorders
and Deaf Education
Lamar Station, Box 10076
Beaumont, TX 77710
www.lamar.edu

Our Lady of the Lake
University
Communication and Learning
Disorders
411 SW 24th St.
San Antonio, TX 78207
www.ollusa.edu

Stephen F. Austin State
University
Communication Sciences and
Disorders Program
P.O. Box 13019 SFA
Nacogdoches, TX 75962
www.sfasu.edu

Texas A & M
University–Kingsville
Program in Communication
Sciences and Disorders
MSC 178, 700 University
Blvd.
Kingsville, TX 78363
www.tamuk.edu

Texas Christian University
Department of
Communication Sciences
and Disorders
TCU Box 297450
Fort Worth, TX 76129
www.csd.tcu.edu

Texas State University
Department of
Communication Disorders
601 University Dr.
San Marcos, TX 78666-4616
www.health.txstate.edu/cdis/
cdis.html

Texas Tech University
Health Sciences Center
Department of Speech,
Language, and Hearing
Sciences
STOP 6073, 3601 4th St.
Lubbock, TX 79430
www.ttuhsc.edu/sah

Texas Woman's University
Department of
Communication Sciences
and Disorders
TWU Station, Box 425737
Denton, TX 76204-5737
www.twu.edu

University of Houston
Program in Communication
Disorders
100 Clinical Research Services
Houston, TX 77204-6018
www.class.uh.edu/comd

University of North Texas
Department of Speech and
   Hearing Sciences
P.O. Box 305010
Denton, TX 76203-5010
www.sphs.unt.edu

University of Texas–Austin
Communication Sciences and
   Disorders
1 University Station, A1100
Austin, TX 78712-1089
http://csd.utexas.edu

University of Texas–Dallas
Program in Communication
   Disorders
UTD Callier Center for
   Communication Disorders
1966 Inwood Rd.
Dallas, TX 75235-7298
www.utdallas.edu/dept/hd

University of Texas–El Paso
Department of Speech-
   Language Pathology
1101 N. Campbell St.
El Paso, TX 79902
www.utep.edu

University of Texas–Pan
   American
Department of
   Communication Sciences
   and Disorders
1201 W. University Dr.
Edinburg, TX 78541
www.panam.edu/dept/
   commdisorder

West Texas A & M University
Program in Communication
   Disorders
P.O. Box 60757
Canyon, TX 79016-0001
www.wtamu.edu

Utah

Brigham Young University
Department of Audiology and
   Speech-Language
   Pathology
136 TLRB
Provo, UT 84602
www.byu.edu

University of Utah
Department of
   Communication Sciences
   and Disorders
390 S. 1530 East
Room #1201 BEH SCI
Salt Lake City, UT 84112-
   0252
www.health.utah.edu/cmdis

Utah State University
Department of
   Communicative Disorders
   and Deaf Education
1000 Old Main Hill
Logan, UT 84322-1000
www.coe.usu.edu/comd/
   index.html

Vermont

University of Vermont
Communication Sciences
Pomeroy Hall
489 Main St.
Burlington, VT 05405-0010
www.uvm.edu/~cmsi

Virginia

Hampton University
Department of
   Communicative Sciences
   and Disorders
Hampton, VA 23668
www.hamptonu.edu

James Madison University
Communication Sciences and
   Disorders
MSC 4304
Harrisonburg, VA 22807
www.jmu.edu

Longwood University
Communication Disorders
Department of Education,
   Special Education, and
   Social Work
201 High St., Hull Bldg.
Farmville, VA 23901
www.longwood.edu
(Accreditation candidate in
   speech-language pathology,
   master's program)

Old Dominion University
Speech-Language Pathology
Child Study Center
Norfolk, VA 23529-0136
www.odu.edu

Radford University
Department of
   Communication Sciences
   and Disorders
P.O. Box 6961
Radford, VA 24142
www.radford.edu

University of Virginia
Communication Disorders
   Program
2205 Fontaine Ave., Ste. 202
P.O. Box 800781
Charlottesville, VA 22908
www.virginia.edu

Washington

Eastern Washington
   University
Department of
   Communication Disorders
Communications Bldg. 108
Cheney, WA 99004-2408
www.ewu.edu

University of Washington
Department of Speech and
   Hearing Sciences
1417 NE 42nd St.
Seattle, WA 98105-6246
www.washington.edu

Washington State University
Department of Speech and
   Hearing Sciences
201 Daggy Hall, Box 642420
Pullman, WA 99164-2420
www.wsu.edu

Western Washington
   University
Department of
   Communication Sciences
   and Disorders
Parks Hall 17, M.S. 9078
Bellingham, WA 98225-9078
www.wwu.edu/~csd

West Virginia

Marshall University
Department of
   Communication Disorders
1 John Marshall Dr.
Huntington, WV 25755-2675
www.marshall.edu/commdis

West Virginia University
Department of Speech
   Pathology and Audiology
805 Allen Hall, Box 6122
Morgantown, WV 26506
www.wvu.edu/~speechpa

Wisconsin

Marquette University
Department of Speech-
  Language Pathology and
  Audiology
P.O. Box 1881
Milwaukee, WI 53233-1881
www.marquette.edu/chs/sppa

University of Wisconsin
Department of
  Communication Disorders
105 Garfield Ave.
Eau Claire, WI 54702-4004
www.uwec.edu/csd

University of Wisconsin
Department of
  Communicative Disorders
1975 Willow Dr.,
  Goodnight Hall
Madison, WI 53706
www.comdis.wisc.edu

University of Wisconsin
Department of
  Communication Sciences
  and Disorders
P.O. Box 413
Milwaukee, WI 53201-0413
www.uwm.edu

University of Wisconsin
Department of
  Communicative Disorders
401 S. Third St.
River Falls, WI 54022-5001
www.uwrf.edu

University of Wisconsin
School of Communicative
  Disorders
1901 4th Ave.
Stevens Point, WI 54481
www.uwsp.edu/commd

University of Wisconsin
Center for Communicative
  Disorders
1011 Roseman Bldg., 800 W.
  Main St.
Whitewater, WI 53190-1790
http://academics.uww.edu/
  commdis

Wyoming

University of Wyoming
Division of Communication
  Disorders
University Station, P.O. Box
  3311
Laramie, WY 82071
www.uwyo.edu/comdis

Minority Schools and Programs

Historically African-American Colleges and Universities

Program names followed by an asterisk (*) are graduate programs; others are preprofessional programs.

Alabama A & M University
Department of Counseling
and Special Education
Communication Sciences and
Disorders Program*
P.O. Box 580
Normal, AL 35762
www.aamu.edu

Elizabeth City State
University
Language, Literature, and
Communication
Department
P.O. Box 958
1704 Weeksville Rd.
Elizabeth City, NC 27909
www.ecsu.edu

Grambling State University
Speech and Hearing Clinic
P.O. Box 803
Grambling, LA 71245
www.gram.edu

Hampton University
Department of
  Communicative Sciences
  and Disorders*
Hampton, VA 23668
www.hamptonu.edu

Howard University
School of Communications
Department of
  Communication Sciences
  and Disorders*
Speech and Hearing Clinic
525 Bryant St. NW
Washington, DC 20059
www.howard.edu/school
  communications/csd/
  about.htm

Jackson State University
Department of Speech and
  Dramatic Art
3825 Ridgewood Rd., Box 23
Jackson, MS 39211
www.jsums.edu

Norfolk State University
Communication Sciences and
  Disorders Program
700 Park Ave.
Norfolk, VA 23504
www.nsu.edu

North Carolina Central
  University
Department of
  Communication Disorders*
P.O. Box 19776
Durham, NC 27707
www.nccu.edu/soe/depart
  ments/communications/
  communication_index.htm

Shaw University
Department of Allied Health
  Professions, Speech
  Pathology, and Audiology
118 E. South St.
Raleigh, NC 27611
www.shawu.edu

South Carolina State
  University
Department of Speech
  Pathology and Audiology*
P.O. Box 7427
300 College St. NE
Orangeburg, SC 29117
www.scsu.edu

Southern University A & M
College
Department of Speech
Pathology and Audiology*
231 Augustus C. Blanks Hall
P.O. Box 9227
Baton Rouge, LA 70813
www.subr.edu

Tennessee State University
Department of Speech
Pathology and Audiology*
330 Tenth Ave. North
P.O. Box 131
Nashville, TN 37203-3401
www.tnstate.edu

University of the District of
Columbia
Department of Languages and
Communication Disorders*
4200 Connecticut Ave. NW,
Bldg. 41, Rm. 413-03
Washington, DC 20008
www.udc.edu

Xavier University
Communications Department
1 Drexel Dr.
New Orleans, LA 70125
www.xula.edu

Minority/Bilingual Emphasis Programs

Arizona State University
Bilingual Training Program
Department of Speech and
Hearing Science
Infant Child Research
Program
P.O. Box 871908
Tempe, AZ 85287-1908
www.asu.edu/clas/shs

California State
University–Long Beach
Cultural/Linguistic Program
Emphasis with Bilingual
Options
Communicative Disorders
Department
1250 Bellflower Blvd.
Long Beach, CA 90840-2501
www.csulb.edu/depts/comm-
disorders/index.html

Florida International
University
Cultural Linguistic Diversity
Infusion and a Bilingual
Specialty Track
Department of
Communication Sciences
and Disorders,
HLS 146-UP
School of Health Sciences
Miami, FL 33199
http://chua2.fiu.edu/csd

Howard University
Leadership Preparation in
Communication Disorders
and Cultural Diversity:
Interdisciplinary Training
for Maternal and Child
Health
School of Communications
Department of
Communication Sciences
and Disorders
Speech and Hearing Clinic
525 Bryant St. NW
Washington, DC 20059
www.howard.edu

Howard University
Multicultural 2000 Project:
Training Speech-Language
Pathologists to Serve
Multicultural Populations
School of Communications
Department of
Communication Sciences
and Disorders
525 Bryant St. NW
Washington, DC 20059
www.howard.edu

Long Island
University–Brooklyn
Campus
Speech-Language Pathology,
Bilingual/Multicultural
Emphasis
Bilingual Specialization
Bilingual Extension to the
New York State Teacher of
Students with Speech and
Language Disabilities
Department of
Communication Sciences
and Disorders
1 University Plaza
Brooklyn, NY 11201-9282
www.brooklyn.liu.edu

Marquette University
Bilingual English-Spanish
  Certificate (BIES) in
  Speech-Language
  Pathology
Department of Speech
  Pathology and Audiology
P.O. Box 1881
Milwaukee, WI 53201-1881
www.marquette.edu/chs/sppa

Nazareth College
Speciality Preparation for
  Speech-Language
  Pathologists to Work with
  Deaf and Hard-of-Hearing
  Children and Youth
Department of
  Communication Sciences
  and Disorders
4245 East Ave.
Rochester, NY 14618
www.ntid.rit.edu/spslp

New Mexico State University
Bilingual Program in Speech-
  Language Pathology
Department of Special
  Education/Communication
  Disorders
Box 30001, 3SPE
Las Cruces, NM 88003-0001
www.nmsu.edu

Saint John's University
Bilingual Extension to the
  M.A. Degree or to the
  New York State Teacher of
  the Speech and Hearing
  Handicapped Certificate
Graduate Program in Speech-
  Language Pathology and
  Audiology
8000 Utopia Pkwy.
Jamaica, NY 11439
www.stjohns.edu

Saint Louis University
Training Early Intervention
  and Preschool Personnel
Preparation of Personnel for
  Careers in Special
  Education
Department of
  Communication Sciences
  and Disorders
McGannon Hall 23
3750 Lindell Blvd.
St. Louis, MO 63108
ww.slu.edu/colleges/cops/cd

San Diego State University
Bilingual Certificate Program
  in Speech-Language
  Pathology
Department of
  Communicative Disorders
5500 Campanile Dr.
San Diego, CA 92182-1518
http://slhs.sdsu.edu/index.php

San Jose State University
Bilingual Speech-Language
  Pathology Program for
  Bilingual Students
Department of
  Communicative Disorders
  and Sciences
College of Education
1 Washington Sq.
San Jose, CA 95192-0079
www.sjsu.edu

Teachers College, Columbia
  University
Bilingual/Bicultural Emphasis
  Track
Bilingual Extension Institute
Department of Biobehavioral
  Studies
525 W. 120th St., Box 180
New York, NY 10027
www.tc.columbia.edu

Temple University
Hispanic Emphasis Program
Department of
  Communication Sciences
110 Weiss Hall (265-62)
Philadelphia, PA 19122
www.temple.edu/commsci

Texas Christian University
Graduate Studies in
  Bilingual/Bicultural
  Speech-Language
  Pathology
Department of
  Communication Sciences
  and Disorders
TCU Box 297450
Fort Worth, TX 76129
www.csd.tcu.edu

Texas State University
Bilingual (English/Spanish)
  and Multicultural Cognates
  in Communication
  Disorders
Department of
  Communication Disorders
601 University Dr.
San Marcos, TX 78666
www.health.txstate.edu/cdis/
  cdis.html

University of Arizona
American Indian Professional
  Training in Speech
  Pathology and Audiology
Department of Speech and
  Hearing Sciences
P.O. Box 210071
Tucson, AZ 85721-0071
http://slhs.arizona.edu

University of Illinois–Urbana
Multicultural Doctoral
  Program (MDP)
Department of Speech and
  Hearing Science
220 Speech and Hearing
  Science Building
901 S. 6th St.
Champaign, IL 61820
www.shs.uiuc.edu

University of Kansas
Project Circle
Native American Training
  Program in Speech-
  Language Pathology and
  Audiology
Department of Speech-
  Language-Hearing Sciences
  and Disorders
3001 Dole Center
1000 Sunnyside Ave.
Lawrence, KS 66045-7555
www.ku.edu/~splh/ipcd

University of Minnesota
Bilingual and Multicultural
  Emphasis
Department of
  Communication Disorders
115 Shevlin Hall
164 Pillsbury Dr. SE
Minneapolis, MN 55455
www.slhs.umn.edu

University of Texas–Austin
Bilingual Communication
  Disorders Project
Department of
  Communication Sciences
  and Disorders
Austin, TX 78712-1089
http://csd.utexas.edu

University of Texas–El Paso
Bilingual Certification
  Program in Speech-
  Language Pathology
  (English/Spanish)
1101 N. Campbell
El Paso, TX 79902
www.utep.edu

University of Texas–Pan
  American
Bilingual Emphasis Program
  in Communication
  Disorders
Department of
  Communication Disorders
1201 University Dr.
Edinburg, TX 78539
www.panam.edu/dept/
  commdisorder

Washington State University
Cultural Interfacing:
  Preparation of Personnel to
  Work with Native
  Americans
Department of Speech and
  Hearing Sciences
201 Daggy Hall, P.O. Box
  642420
Pullman, WA 99164-2420
www.wsu.edu

Appendix C

Canadian Training Programs

Dalhousie University
School of Human
   Communication Disorders
5599 Fenwick St.
Halifax, NS B3H 4R2
www.dal.ca

McGill University
School of Communication
   Sciences and Disorders
Beatty Hall
1266 Pine Ave. West
Montreal, QC H3G 1A8
www.mcgill.ca

University of Alberta
Department of Speech
   Pathology and Audiology
2-70 Corbett Hall
Edmonton, AL T6G 2G4
www.ualberta.ca

University of British
   Columbia
School of Audiology and
   Speech Science
5804 Fairview Ave.
Vancouver, BC V6T 1Z3
www.ubc.ca

Université Laval
Programme de Maîtrise en
  Orthophonie
Pavillion Vandry
Québec, G1K 7P4
www.ulaval.ca

Université de Montréal
École d'Orthophonie et
  d'Audiologie
Faculté de Médecine
CP 6128, Station Centre-Ville
Montréal, QC H3C 3J7
www.umontreal.ca

Université d'Ottawa
Programme d'Audiologie et
  d'Orthophonie
École des Sciences de la
  Réadaption
Faculté des Sciences de la
  Santé
451 Chemin Smyth
Ottawa, ON K1N 8M5
www.uottawa.ca

University of Toronto
Department of Speech-
  Language Pathology
Rehabilitation Sciences
  Building
500 University Ave., Rm. 160
Toronto, ON M5G 1V7
www.utoronto.ca

University of Western Ontario
School of Communicative
  Disorders
Elborn College
London, ON N6G 1H1
www.uwo.ca

U.S. State Listing of Board of Examiners

Alabama

Alabama Board of Examiners
for Speech Pathology and
Audiology
P.O. Box 304760
Montgomery, AL 36104
www.abespa.org

Alaska

Alaska Division of
Occupational Licensing
P.O. Box 110806
Juneau, AK 99811-0806
www.dced.state.ak.us/occ

Arizona

Arizona Department of
Health Services
Office of Special Licensing
150 N. 18th, Ste. 460
Phoenix, AZ 85007
www.hs.state.az.us

Arkansas

Arkansas Board of Examiners
for Speech and Audiology
101 E. Capitol, Ste. 211
Little Rock, AR 72201
www.abespa.com

California

California Speech-Language
Pathology and Audiology
Board
1422 Howe Ave., Ste. 3
Sacramento, CA 95825-3204
www.dca.ca.gov/slpab

Colorado

(No license required for speech-language pathologists)

Connecticut

Connecticut SLP and
Audiology Licensure
Department of Public Health
410 Capitol Ave., MS
#12APP
P.O. Box 340308
Hartford, CT 06134-0308
www.state.ct.us/dph

Delaware

Delaware Audiology, SLP, and
Hearing Aid Dispensing
Board
861 Silver Lake Blvd.
Canon Bldg., Ste. 203
Dover, DE 19904
www.professionallicensing
.state.de.us

District of Columbia

District of Columbia Board of
Speech Therapy
614 H St. NW, Rm. 923
Washington, DC 20001

Florida

Florida Board of Speech
Language Pathology and
Audiology
4052 Bald Cypress Way,
Bin C06
Tallahassee, FL 32399
www.doh.state.fl.us/mqa

Georgia

Georgia Board of Examiners
for Speech-Language
Pathology and Audiology
237 Coliseum Dr.
Macon, GA 31217
www.sos.state.ga.us/plb/speech

Hawaii

Hawaii Board of Speech
Pathology and Audiology
Department of Commerce
and Consumer Affairs
P.O. Box 3469
Honolulu, HI 96801
www.state.hi.us/dcca

Idaho

Idaho State Board of Speech
Therapy Examiners
Bureau of Occupational
Licensing
1109 Main St., Ste. 220
Boise, ID 83702
www.sco.state.id.us

Illinois

Illinois Department of
Professional Regulations
320 W. Washington St.
Springfield, IL 62786
www.dpr.state.il.us

Indiana

Indiana Speech-Language
Pathology and Audiology
Board
Indiana Health Profession
Service Bureau
402 W. Washington St.,
Rm. W066
Indianapolis, IN 46204-2758
www.in.gov/hpb/boards/slpab

Iowa

Iowa State Board of SLP and
Audiology Examiners
Bureau of Professional
Licensure
Lucas State Office Bldg.
321 E. 12th St., 5th Fl.
Des Moines, IA 50319-0075
www.idph.state.ia.us

Kansas

Kansas Department of Health
and Environment
Health Occupations
Credentialing
1000 SW Jackson, Ste. 200
Topeka, KS 66612-1365
www.kdheks.gov

Kentucky

Kentucky Board of Speech-
Language Pathology and
Audiology
P.O. Box 1360
Frankfort, KY 40602-1360
www.state.ky.us

Louisiana

Louisiana Board of Examiners
for Speech-Language
Pathology and Audiology
18550 Highland Rd., Ste. B
Baton Rouge, LA 70809
www.lbespa.org

Maine

Maine Board of Examiners on
Speech Pathology and
Audiology
35 State House Station
Augusta, ME 04333
www.state.me.us/pfr/olr/
categories/cat41.htm

Maryland

Maryland Board of Examiners
for Audiology, Hearing Aid
Dispensers, and Speech-
Language Pathologists
4201 Patterson Ave.
Baltimore, MD 21215
www.mdboardaudhadslp.org

Massachusetts

Massachusetts Board of
Speech-Language
Pathology and Audiology
239 Causeway St., Ste. 500
Boston, MA 02114
www.mass.gov/dpl/boards/sp

Michigan

(Only regulates audiology)

Minnesota

Minnesota Department of
  Health
Speech-Language Pathology
  and Audiology Advisory
  Council
85 E. 7th Pl.
St. Paul, MN 55164
www.health.state.mn.us

Mississippi

Mississippi State Department
  of Health, Professional
  Licensure
570 E. Woodrow Wilson Dr.
Jackson, MS 39216
www.msdh.state.ms.us

Missouri

Missouri Board of
  Registration for the
  Healing Arts
Advisory Commission of
  Professional Speech-
  Language Pathologists and
  Audiologists
3605 Missouri Blvd.
Jefferson City, MO 65102
www.pr.mo.gov/healingarts

Montana

Montana Board of Speech-
  Language Pathologists and
  Audiologists
301 S. Park, 4th Fl.
Helena, MT 59620
www.state.mt.us

Nebraska

Nebraska Board of Audiology
  and Speech-Language
  Pathology
P.O. Box 94986
301 Centennial Mall South
Lincoln, NE 68509
www.hhs.state.ne.us

Nevada

Nevada State Board of
  Examiners for Audiology
  and Speech Pathology
P.O. Box 70550
Reno, NV 89570-0550
http://speech_pathology.state
  .nv.us

New Hampshire

New Hampshire Allied Health
  Board
2 Industrial Park Dr.
Concord, NH 03301-8520
www.nh.gov/alliedhealth/
  boards

New Jersey

New Jersey Audiology and
  Speech-Language Advisory
  Committee
124 Halsey St., 6th Fl.
Newark, NJ 07102
www.state.nj.us

New Mexico

New Mexico SLP, Audiology,
  and Hearing Aid
  Dispensers Practices Board
P.O. Box 25101
Santa Fe, NM 87504
www.rld.state.nm.us/b&c/
  speech

New York

New York State Board for
  Speech-Language
  Pathology and Audiology
Education Bldg., 2nd Fl.,
  West Wing
Albany, NY 12234
www.op.nysed.gov

North Carolina

North Carolina Board of
  Examiners for Speech-
  Language Pathology and
  Audiology
P.O. Box 16885
Greensboro, NC 27416
www.ncboeslpa.org

North Dakota

North Dakota Board of
  Examiners on Audiology
  and SLP
Bureau of Educational
  Services and Applied
  Research
P.O. Box 7189
Grand Forks, ND 58202
www.governor.state.nd.us/
  boards

Ohio

Ohio Board of SLP and
Audiology
77 S. High St., 16th Fl.
Columbus, OH 43266
www.slpaud.ohio.gov

Oklahoma

Oklahoma State Board of
Examiners for SLP and
Audiology
P.O. Box 53592
Oklahoma City, OK 73152
www.oklaosf.state.ok.us

Oregon

Oregon Board of Examiners
for Speech-Language
Pathology and Audiology
800 NE Oregon St., Ste. 407
Portland, OR 97232
www.oregon.gov

Pennsylvania

Pennsylvania Board of
Examiners for Speech-
Language and Hearing
Bureau of Professional and
Occupational Affairs
P.O. Box 2649
Harrisburg, PA 17105-2649
www.dos.state.pa.us

Rhode Island

Rhode Island Board of
Examiners in SLP and
Audiology
Rhode Island Department of
Health
3 Capitol Hill, Rm. 104
Providence, RI 02908-5097

South Carolina

South Carolina Board of
Examiners in Speech
Pathology and Audiology
P.O. Box 11329, Ste. 101
Columbia, SC 29211
www.llr.state.sc.us

South Dakota

(Only regulates audiology)

Tennessee

Tennessee State Board of
Communication Disorders
and Sciences
Speech Pathology and
Audiology
425 5th Ave. North, 1st Fl.
Nashville, TN 37247
www.state.tn.us

Texas

Texas Department of State
Health Services
1100 W. 49th St.
Austin, TX 78756-3183
www.dshs.state.tx.us/plc

Utah

Utah Speech-Language
Pathology and Audiology
Licensing Board
P.O. Box 146741
Salt Lake City, UT 84114-
6741
www.dopl.utah.gov/licensing/
speech_pathology_and
_audiology.html

Vermont

Vermont Department of
Education
120 State St.
Montpelier, VT 05620-2501
www.doe.state.vt.us

Virginia

Virginia State Board of
Audiology and Speech
Pathology
6606 W. Broad St., 4th Fl.
Richmond, VA 23230-1717
www.dhp.state.va.us

Washington

Washington Department of
  Health
1300 SE Quince St.
P.O. Box 47869
Olympia, WA 98504-7869
https://fortress.wa.gov/doh/
  hpqa1/hps7/hearing
  _speech/default.htm

West Virginia

West Virginia Board of
  Examiners for SLP and
  Audiology
HC 78, Box 9A
Troy, WV 26443
www.wvspeechandaudiology
  .org/index.htm

Wisconsin

Wisconsin Council on SLP
  and Audiology
Department of Regulation
  and Licensing
P.O. Box 8935
Madison, WI 53708-8935
www.wisha.org

Wyoming

Wyoming Board of Speech-
  Language Pathology and
  Audiology
2020 Carey Ave., Ste. 201
Cheyenne, WY 82002
http://plboards.state.wy.us/
  speech

Appendix E

U.S. State Education Agencies

Alabama

Alabama Department of
 Education
Division of Special Education
50 N. Ripley St.
Montgomery, AL 36130-3901
www.alsde.edu

Alaska

Alaska Department of
 Education
Office of Special Education
 Services
801 W. 10th St., Ste. 200
Juneau, AK 99801
www.eed.state.ak.us

Arizona

Arizona Department of
 Education
Exceptional Student Services
1535 W. Jefferson
Phoenix, AZ 85007
www.ade.state.az.us

Arkansas

Special Education Unit
4 Capitol Mall
Little Rock, AR 72201
http://arksped.k12.ar.us

California

California Department of
   Education
Special Education Division
P.O. Box 944272
Sacramento, CA 94244
www.cde.ca.gov

Colorado

Colorado Department of
   Education
Communication Disorders
   and Special Education
   Services
State Office Bldg.
201 E. Colfax Ave.
Denver, CO 80203-1799
www.cde.state.co.us

Connecticut

Connecticut Department of
   Education
Bureau of Special Education
Speech-Language Pathology
165 Capitol Ave.
Hartford, CT 06145-2219
www.po.state.ct.us

Delaware

Exceptional Children Special
   Program Division
P.O. Box 1402
Dover, DE 19903
www.doe.state.de.us/
   programs/specialed

District of Columbia

Office of Special Education
825 N. Capitol St. NE,
   6th Fl.
Washington, DC 20002
http://seo.dc.gov

Florida

Florida Department of
   Education
Bureau of Education for
   Exceptional Students
Speech and Language
   Impaired/Deaf and Hard
   of Hearing
325 W. Gaines St.
Tallahassee, FL 32399-0400
www.fldoe.org

Georgia

Georgia Department of
Education
Speech-Language Disorders
Program
State Office Bldg.
1870 Twin Towers East
Atlanta, GA 30334-5040
http://public.doe.k12.ga.us

Hawaii

Hawaii Department of
Education
Special Education Section
Speech/Language/Hearing
3430 Leahi Ave.
Honolulu, HI 96815
http://doe.k12.hi.us

Idaho

State Department of
Education
650 W. State St.
P.O. Box 83720
Boise, ID 83720-0027
www.sde.state.id.us

Illinois

Illinois State Board of
Education
Center for Educational
Innovation and Reform
100 N. First St.
Springfield, IL 62777
www.isbe.state.il.us

Indiana

Indiana Department of
Education
Division of Special Education
Center for Community
Relations and Special
Education
State House, Rm. 229
Indianapolis, IN 46204
www.doe.state.in.us

Iowa

Iowa Department of
Education
Hearing
Conservation/Education
Services
Grimes State Office Bldg.
Des Moines, IA 50319-0146
www.state.ia.us/educate

Kansas

Kansas Board of Education
Special Outcomes Team
120 E. 10th Ave.
Topeka, KS 66612
www.ksbe.state.ks.us

Kentucky

Kentucky Department of
    Education
Office of Education for
    Exceptional Children
Capital Plaza Tower, Rm. 820
Frankfort, KY 40601
www.education.ky.gov

Louisiana

Louisiana Department of
    Education
Bureau of Appraisal and
    Support Services
Office of Special Education
P.O. Box 94064
Baton Rouge, LA 70804-9064
www.doe.state.la.us/lde

Maine

Maine Department of
    Education
Office of Special Services
State House Station, #23
Augusta, ME 04333
www.state.me.us/education

Maryland

Maryland Department of
    Education
Division of Special Education
200 W. Baltimore St.
Baltimore, MD 21202-2595
www.marylandpublic
    schools.org

Massachusetts

Massachusetts Department of
    Education
Division of Special Education
1385 Hancock St.
Quincy, MA 02169-5183
www.doe.mass.edu

Michigan

Michigan Department of
Education
Office of Special Education
and Early Intervention
Services
608 W. Allegan
Lansing, MI 48993
www.michigan.gov/mde

Minnesota

Minnesota Department of
Education
Instructional Improvement
818 Capitol Sq.
St. Paul, MN 55101
http://education.state.mn.us

Mississippi

Mississippi Department of
Education
Office of Special Education
P.O. Box 771
Jackson, MS 39205-0771
www.mde.k12.ms.us

Missouri

Missouri Department of
Elementary-Secondary
Education
Division of Special Education
P.O. Box 480
Jefferson City, MO 65102
www.dese.state.mo.us

Montana

Montana Office of Public
Instruction
Department of Special
Education
P.O. Box 202501
State Capitol
Helena, MT 59620-2501
www.opi.state.mt.us

Nebraska

Nebraska Department of
Education
Speech/Language Programs
Special Education Office
6949 S. 110th St.
Omaha, NE 68128
www.nde.state.ne.us

Nevada

Nevada Department of
Education
4604 Carriage La.
Las Vegas, NV 89119
www.doe.nv.gov

New Hampshire

New Hampshire Department
of Education
Bureau of Special Education
101 Pleasant St.
Concord, NH 03301-3860
www.ed.state.nh.us/education

New Jersey

New Jersey Department of
Education
Division of Special Education
P.O. Box CN 500
225 W. State St.
Trenton, NJ 08625-0001
www.state.nj.us/education

New Mexico

New Mexico State Public
Education Department
Special Education Unit
300 Don Gaspar Ave.
Santa Fe, NM 87501-2786
www.ped.state.nm.us

New York

New York Department of
Education
Vocational and Educational
Services for Individuals
with Disabilities
1 Commerce Plaza
Albany, NY 12234
www.nysed.gov

North Carolina

North Carolina State
Department of Public
Instruction
Division of Exceptional
Children
310 N. Wilmington St.
Raleigh, NC 27601
www.ncpublicschools.org

North Dakota

North Dakota Department of
Public Instruction
600 E. Boulevard Ave.,
Dept. 201
Bismarck, ND 58505-0440
www.dpi.state.nd.us

Ohio

Ohio Department of
Education
Office for Exceptional
Children
25 S. Front St.
Columbus, OH 43215
www.ode.state.oh.us

Oklahoma

Oklahoma Department of
Education
Special Education Section
2500 N. Lincoln Blvd.
Oklahoma City, OK 73105-
4599
www.sde.state.ok.us

Oregon

Oregon Department of
Education
Office of Special Education
255 Capitol Ave. NE
Salem, OR 97310-0203
www.ode.state.or.us

Pennsylvania

Pennsylvania Department of
Education
Office of Special Needs
333 Market St.
Harrisburg, PA 17126
www.pde.state.pa.us

Rhode Island

Rhode Island Department of
Education
Office of Special Needs
255 Westminster St.
Providence, RI 02903
www.ridoe.net

South Carolina

South Carolina Department of
Education
Office of Exceptional
Children
1429 Senate St.
503 Rutledge Bldg.
Columbia, SC 29201-6123
www.myscschools.com

South Dakota

South Dakota Department of
Education
Section for Special Education
700 Governor's Dr.
Pierre, SD 57501
http://doe.sd.gov

Tennessee

Tennessee Department of
Education
Division for Special Education
Andrew Johnson Tower,
6th Fl.
Nashville, TN 37243-0375
www.state.tn.us/education

Texas

Texas Education Agency
Special Education Division
1701 N. Congress
Austin, TX 78701
www.tea.state.tx.us

Utah

Utah State Office of
Education
Specialist Communication
Disorders and Learning
Disabilities
Special Education Services
Unit
250 E. 500 South
Salt Lake City, UT 84114-
4200
www.usoe.k12.ut.us

Vermont

Vermont Department of
Education
Speech, Language, and
Hearing Services
Special Education Division
120 State St.
Montpelier, VT 05620-2501
www.state.vt.us/educ

Virginia

Virginia Department of
    Education
Division of Special Education
    and Student Services
P.O. Box 2120
Richmond, VA 23210-2120
www.pen.k12.va.us

Washington

Special Education Washington
    Department of Public
    Instruction
Old Capitol Bldg.
P.O. Box 47200
Olympia, WA 98504-7200
www.sbe.wa.gov

West Virginia

West Virginia Department of
    Education
Office of Special Education
1900 Kanawha Blvd. East
Bldg. #6, Rm. 304
Charleston, WV 25305
www.wvde.state.wv.us

Wisconsin

Wisconsin Department of
    Public Instruction and
    Special Education
125 S. Webster St., 4th Fl.
Madison, WI 53707-7841
http://dpi.wi.gov

Wyoming

Wyoming Department of
    Education
Special Education
2300 Capitol Ave.
Hathaway Bldg., 2nd Fl.
Cheyenne, WY 82002-0050
www.k12.wy.us

Appendix F

U.S. and Canadian Speech-Language-Hearing Associations

U.S. Associations

Alabama

Speech and Hearing
Association of Alabama
P.O. Box 130220
Birmingham, AL 35213
www.alabamashaa.org

Alaska

Alaska Speech-Language-
Hearing Association
4325 Laurel St., Ste. 100
Anchorage, AK 99508
www.aksha.org

Arizona

Arizona Speech-Language-
Hearing Association
P.O. Box 30988
Phoenix, AZ 85046
www.arsha.org

Arkansas

Arkansas Speech-Language-
Hearing Association
P.O. Box 250261
Little Rock, AR 72225-0261
www.arksha.org

California

California Speech-Language-
Hearing Association
825 University Ave.
Sacramento, CA 95825
www.csha.org

Colorado

Colorado Speech-Language-
Hearing Association
P.O. Box 345
Sedalia, CO 80135
www.cshassoc.org

Connecticut

Connecticut Speech-
Language-Hearing
Association, Inc.
213 Back La.
Newington, CT 06111-4204
www.ctspeechhearing.org

Delaware

Delaware Speech-Language-
Hearing Association, Inc.
P.O. Box 7383
Newark, DE 19711
www.dsha.org

District of Columbia

District of Columbia Speech-
Language-Hearing
Association
P.O. Box 29590
Washington, DC 20017
www.dcsha.org

Florida

Florida Association of Speech-
Language Pathologists and
Audiologists
222 S. Westmonte Dr.,
Ste. 101
Altamonte Springs, FL 32714
www.flasha.org

Georgia

Georgia Speech-Language-
Hearing Association
20423 State Rd. 7,
Ste. F6-491
Boca Raton, FL 33498
www.gsha.org

Hawaii

Hawaii Speech-Language-
Hearing Association
P.O. Box 235850
Honolulu, HI 96823-3514
www.hsha.org

Idaho

Idaho School for the Deaf
and Blind
1450 Main St.
Gooding, ID 83330
www.idahosha.org

Illinois

Illinois Speech-Language-
Hearing Association
230 E. Ohio St., Ste. 400
Chicago, IL 60611-3265
www.ishail.org

Indiana

Indiana Speech-Language-
Hearing Association
1 N. Capitol Ave., Ste. 1111
Indianapolis, IN 46204
www.islha.org

Iowa

Iowa Speech-Language-
Hearing Association
525 SW 5th St., Ste. A
Des Moines, IA 50309
www.isha.org

Kansas

Kansas Speech-Language-
Hearing Association
3900 17th Ave.
Great Bend, KS 67530
www.ksha.org

Kentucky

Kentucky Speech-Language-
Hearing Association
535 W. 2nd St., Ste. 103
Lexington, KY 40508
www.kysha.org

Louisiana

Louisiana Speech-Language-
Hearing Association
8550 United Plaza Blvd.,
Ste. 1001
Baton Rouge, LA 70809
www.lsha.org

Maine

Maine Speech-Language-
Hearing Association
381 Mann Hill Rd.
Holden, ME 04429
www.mslha.org

Maryland

Maryland Speech-Language-
Hearing Association
P.O. Box 31
Manchester, MD 21102
www.mdslha.org

Massachusetts

Massachusetts Speech-
Language-Hearing
Association
77 Rumford Ave., Ste. 3B
Waltham, MA 02453
www.mshahearsay.org

Michigan

Michigan Speech-Language-
Hearing Association
790 W. Lake Lansing Rd.,
Ste. 500-A
East Lansing, MI 48823
www.michiganspeech
hearing.org

Minnesota

Minnesota Speech-Language-
Hearing Association
P.O. Box 26115
St. Louis Park, MN 55426
www.msha.net

Mississippi

Mississippi Speech-Language-
Hearing Association
P.O. Box 22664
Jackson, MS 39225-2664
www.mshausa.org

Missouri

Missouri Speech-Language-
Hearing Association
901 Missouri Blvd., PMB 355
Jefferson City, MO 65109-
1759
www.showmemsha.org

Montana

Montana Speech-Language-
Hearing Association
P.O. Box 215
Miles City, MT 59301
www.mshaonline.org

Nebraska

Nebraska Speech-Language-
Hearing Association
455 S. 11th St., Ste. A
Lincoln, NE 68508-2105
www.nslha.org

Nevada

Nevada Speech-Language-
Hearing Association
P.O. Box 7313
Reno, NV 89510-7313
www.nvsha.org

New Hampshire

New Hampshire Speech-
Language-Hearing
Association, Inc.
P.O. Box 1538
Concord, NH 03302-1538
www.nhslha.org

New Jersey

New Jersey Speech-Language-
Hearing Association
203 Towne Centre Dr.
Hillsborough, NJ 08844
www.njsha.org

New Mexico

New Mexico Speech-
Language-Hearing
Association
P.O. Box 66085
Albuquerque, NM 87193-
3580
www.nmsha.net

New York

New York State Speech-
Language-Hearing
Association, Inc.
1 Northway La.
Latham, NY 12110
www.nysslha.org

North Carolina

North Carolina Speech-
Language-Hearing
Association
P.O. Box 28359
Raleigh, NC 27611-8359
www.ncshla.org

North Dakota

North Dakota Speech-
Language-Hearing
Association
P.O. Box 12775
Grand Forks, ND 58208-
2775
www.ndslha.org

Ohio

Ohio Speech-Language-
Hearing Association
P.O. Box 309
Germantown, OH 45327-
0309
www.oshla.org

Oklahoma

Oklahoma Speech-Language-
Hearing Association
P.O. Box 53217
State Capitol Station
Oklahoma City, OK 73105
www.oslha.org

Oregon

Oregon Speech-Language-
Hearing Association
P.O. Box 2042
Salem, OR 97308
www.oregonspeechand
hearing.org

Pennsylvania

Pennsylvania Speech-
Language-Hearing
Association
800 Perry Hwy., Ste. 3
Pittsburgh, PA 15229-1128
www.psha.org

Rhode Island

Rhode Island Speech-
Language-Hearing
Association
P.O. Box 9241
Providence, RI 02940
www.risha.org

South Carolina

South Carolina Speech-
Language-Hearing
Association
701 Gervais St., Ste. 150-206
Columbia, SC 29201
www.scsha.org

South Dakota

South Dakota Speech-
Language-Hearing
Association
P.O. Box 308
Sioux Falls, SD 57101-0308
www.sdslha.org

Tennessee

Tennessee Association of
Audiology and Speech-
Language Pathology
P.O. Box 70
Spring Hill, TN 37174
www.taaslp.org

Texas

Texas Speech-Language-
Hearing Association
P.O. Box 140647
Austin, TX 78714
www.txsha.org

Utah

Utah Speech-Language-
Hearing Association
1379 31st St.
Ogden, UT 84403
www.ushaonline.net

Vermont

Vermont Speech-Language-
Hearing Association, Inc.
P.O. Box 768
Waitsfield, VT 05673
www.vslha.org

Virginia

Speech-Language-Hearing
Association of Virginia,
Inc.
2101 Libbie Ave.
Richmond, VA 23230
www.shav.org

Washington

Washington Speech and
Hearing Association
2150 N. 107th St., Ste. 205
Seattle, WA 98133
www.wslha.org

West Virginia

West Virginia Speech-
Language-Hearing
Association
General Hospital
501 Morris St.
Charleston, WV 25301
www.wvsha.org

Wisconsin

Wisconsin Speech-Language
Pathology and Audiology
Professional Association
P.O. Box 1109
Madison, WI 53701
www.wisha.org

Wyoming

Wyoming Speech-Language-
Hearing Association
760 W. 57th St.
Casper, WY 82601
www.wsha.info

Canadian Associations

Alberta College of Speech-
Language Pathologists and
Audiologists
#209-3132 Parsons Rd.
Edmonton, AB T6N 1L6
www.acslpa.ab.ca

Association of Northwest
Territories Speech-
Language Pathologists and
Audiologists
Speech Pathology Department
Stanton Territorial Hospital
P.O. Box 10, 550 Byrne Rd.
Yellowknife, NT X1A 2N1
www.cicic.ca/professions

Association of Yukon Speech-
Language Pathologists and
Audiologists
Special Programs
Department of Education
P.O. Box 2703
Whitehorse, YT Y1A 2C6
www.cicic.ca/professions

British Columbia Association
of Speech-Language
Pathologists and
Audiologists
402-1755 W. Broadway
Vancouver, BC V6J 4S5
www.bcaslpa.bc.ca

Canadian Association of
Speech-Language
Pathologists and
Audiologists
401-200 Elgin St.
Ottawa, ON K2P 1L5
www.caslpa.ca

Manitoba Speech and Hearing
Association
#2-333 Vaughan St.
Winnipeg, MB R3B 3J9
www.msha.ca

New Brunswick Association of
Speech-Language
Pathologists and
Audiologists
147 Ellerdale Ave.
Moncton, NB E1A 3M8
www.communicationnb.ca

Newfoundland Association of
Speech-Language
Pathologists and
Audiologists
P.O. Box 21212
St. John's, NF A1A 5B2
www.nlaslpa.ca

Ontario Association of
Speech-Language
Pathologists and
Audiologists
410 Jarvis St.
Toronto, ON M4Y 2G6
www.osla.on.ca

Ordre des Orthophonistes et
Audiologistes du Québec
235, René Lévesque est,
Ste. 601
Montréal, QC H2X 1N8
www.ooaq.qc.ca

Prince Edward Island Speech
and Hearing Association
Department of Child and
Family Services
P.O. Box 20076
Charlottetown, PE C1A 9E3
www.cicic.ca/professions

Saskatchewan Association of
Speech-Language
Pathologists and
Audiologists
P.O. Box 3357
Regina, SK S3P 3H1
www.saslpa.ca

Speech and Hearing
Association of Nova Scotia
P.O. Box 775
Halifax Central CRO
Halifax, NS B3J 2V2
www.shans.ca

References

American Hospital Association. *2004 Annual Survey.* Chicago, Ill: American Hospital Association, 2004.

American Speech-Language-Hearing Association. *Incidence and Prevalence of Speech, Voice, and Language Disorders in Adults in the United States.* Rockville, Md.: American Speech-Language-Hearing Association, 2006.

American Speech-Language-Hearing Association. "Basic Requirements for Maintaining CCCs." Rockville, Md.: American Speech-Language-Hearing Association, 2005.

American Speech-Language-Hearing Association. "Become an International Affiliate." Rockville, Md.: American Speech-Language-Hearing Association, 2005.

American Speech-Language-Hearing Association. "Fact Sheet: ASHA Certification Standards." Rockville, Md.: American Speech-Language-Hearing Association, 2005.

American Speech-Language-Hearing Association. "Market Trends." Rockville, Md.: American Speech-Language-Hearing Association, 2005.

American Speech-Language-Hearing Association. "Membership and Certification Manual for ASHA Certification in Accord with ASHA/CASLPA Agreement for Mutual Recognition." Rockville, Md.: American Speech-Language-Hearing Association, 2005.

American Speech-Language-Hearing Association. "Recruitment and Retention of SLPs in Health Care: A Guide for Administrators, Program Directors, and Recruiters." Rockville, Md.: American Speech-Language-Hearing Association, 2005.

American Speech-Language-Hearing Association. "Shortages in Special Education and Related Services Focus of New Coalition—Shortages Outstrip Those in Math, Science." Rockville, Md.: American Speech-Language-Hearing Association, 2005.

American Speech-Language-Hearing Association. *SLP Healthcare Survey 2005*. Rockville, Md.: American Speech-Language-Hearing Association, 2005.

American Speech-Language-Hearing Association. "Special Interest Divisions." Rockville, Md.: American Speech-Language-Hearing Association, 2005.

American Speech-Language-Hearing Association. "National Programs and Activities." Rockville, Md.: American Speech-Language-Hearing Association, 2004.

American Speech-Language-Hearing Association. *Preferred Practice Patterns for the Profession of Speech-Language-Pathology*. Rockville, Md.: American Speech-Language-Hearing Association, 2004.

American Speech-Language-Hearing Association. *2004 Schools Survey.* Rockville, Md.: American Speech-Language-Hearing Association, 2004.

American Speech-Language-Hearing Association. *2003 Omnibus Survey Caseload Report: SLP.* Rockville, Md.: American Speech-Language-Hearing Association, 2003.

American Speech-Language-Hearing Association. *2003 Omnibus Survey Salary Report: Annual Salaries.* Rockville, Md.: American Speech-Language-Hearing Association, 2003.

American Speech-Language-Hearing Association. *ASHA Speech-Language Pathology Health Care Survey.* Rockville, Md.: American Speech-Language-Hearing Association, 2002.

American Speech-Language-Hearing Association. Revisions to the *Membership and Certification Handbook.* In *Membership and Certification Handbook of the American Speech-Language-Hearing Association.* Rockville, Md.: American Speech-Language-Hearing Association, 1998.

American Speech-Language-Hearing Association. "About Our Organization." Rockville, Md.: American Speech-Language-Hearing Association, 1997–2005.

American Speech-Language-Hearing Association. "Employment Settings." Rockville, Md.: American Speech-Language-Hearing Association, 1997–2005.

American Speech-Language-Hearing Association. "Fact Sheet: Speech-Language Pathology." Rockville, Md.: American Speech-Language-Hearing Association, 1997–2005.

American Speech-Language-Hearing Association. "Financial Aid Resources for Students." Rockville, Md.: American Speech-Language-Hearing Association, 1997–2005.

American Speech-Language-Hearing Association. "State Licensure Trends." Rockville, Md.: American Speech-Language-Hearing Association, 1997–2005.

American Speech-Language-Hearing Association. "Successful Strategies for Entry into Graduate Schools in Communication Sciences and Disorders." Rockville, Md.: American Speech-Language-Hearing Association, 1997.

American Speech-Language-Hearing Association. "Standards and Implementation Procedures for the Certificate of Clinical Competence." In *Membership and Certification Handbook of the American Speech-Language-Hearing Association*. Rockville, Md.: American Speech-Language-Hearing Association, 1993.

American Speech-Language-Hearing Association (ASHA) Ad Hoc Committee on Service Delivery in Schools. "Definitions of Communications Disorders and Variations." *ASHA*, 35, 40–41. Rockville, Md.: American Speech-Language-Hearing Association, 1993.

Boswell, S. "Professions on Fast Track for Growth." *The ASHAleader ONLINE*. Rockville, Md.: American Speech-Language-Hearing Association, 2003.

Canadian Association of Speech-Language Pathologists and Audiologists. *CASLPA 2005 Salary Survey*. Ottawa, ON: Canadian Association of Speech-Language Pathologists and Audiologists, 2005.

Canadian Association of Speech-Language Pathologists and Audiologists. "About CASLPA." Ottawa, ON: Canadian Association of Speech-Language Pathologists and Audiologists, 2002.

Canadian Association of Speech-Language Pathologists and
Audiologists. "About Certification." Ottawa, ON: Canadian
Association of Speech-Language Pathologists and
Audiologists, 2002.

Flower, R. M. *Delivery of Speech-Language Pathology and
Audiology Services.* Baltimore: Williams and Wilkins, 1986.

Holland, A., and O. Reinmuth. "Aphasia in Adults." In G. Shames
and N. Anderson (eds.), *Human Communication Disorders: An
Introduction.* Columbus, OH: Charles Merrill, 2002.

Human Resources Development Canada: BC/Yukon Region, and
the BC Ministry of Advanced Education, Training, and
Technology. "Therapy and Assessment Professionals (NOC
314)." In *Work Futures: British Columbia Occupational
Outlook.* Victoria, BC: Human Resources Development
Canada, 2000.

Joss, M. "Careers in: Speech-Language Pathology."
http://www.diversityalliedhealth.com, 2005.

LaPointe, L. "Neurogenic Disorders of Speech." In G. Shames and
N. Anderson (eds.), *Human Communication Disorders: An
Introduction.* Columbus, OH: Charles Merrill, 2002.

Leonard, L. "Early Language Development and Language
Disorders." In G. Shames and N. Anderson (eds.), *Human
Communication Disorders: An Introduction.* Columbus, OH:
Charles Merrill, 2002.

McReynolds, L. V. "Functional Articulation Disorders." In G.
Shames and N. Anderson (eds.), *Human Communication
Disorders: An Introduction.* Columbus, OH: Charles Merrill,
2002.

Moore, P. "Voice Disorders." In G. Shames and N. Anderson (eds.), *Human Communication Disorders: An Introduction.* Columbus, OH: Charles Merrill, 2002.

National Information Center for Children and Youth with Disabilities. "Who's Teaching Our Children with Disabilities?" Washington, DC: National Information Center for Children and Youth with Disabilities, 2000.

National Institute on Deafness and Other Communication Disorders. "Statistics on Voice, Speech, and Language." Bethesda, Md.: National Institute on Deafness and Other Communication Disorders, 2004.

Shames, G. and C. Florence. "Disorders of Fluency." In G. Shames and N. Anderson (eds.), *Human Communication Disorders: An Introduction.* Columbus, OH: Charles Merrill, 2002.

U.S. Bureau of Labor, Bureau of Labor Statistics. "Occupational Employment and Wages: Speech-Language Pathologists." Washington, DC: Bureau of Labor Statistics, 2004.

About the Author

Dr. Patricia Larkins Hicks's professional career in the field of speech-language pathology has afforded her the opportunity to work in a variety of employment settings and engage in many different employment functions (clinician, supervisor, researcher, academician, corporate executive). She began her career at the Easter Seal Speech and Hearing Center (Brunswick, Georgia) providing direct clinical services to a diverse clientele in six rural counties. While there, she assumed administrative duties when she was appointed Head Speech-Language Pathologist.

Later she joined the faculty at Armstrong State College (Savannah, Georgia) and then at Howard University (Washington, DC). At the college and university setting, Hicks directed a university clinic, established a family intervention program, taught both undergraduate and graduate courses, directed research, and assumed a leadership role in obtaining ASHA program accreditation.

At the National Institutes of Health Clinical Center (Bethesda, Maryland), she served as a consultant and conducted research. At the American Speech-Language-Hearing Association (Rockville, Maryland), Hicks served as the director of the Speech-Language Pathology Liaison Branch. In this position, she worked with many association committees in developing position statements, guidelines, and association policies. Additionally, Hicks conducted and evaluated educational programs and products for more than sixty thousand speech-language pathologists.

In the corporate sector, she provided clinical leadership as the vice president of professional services for NovaCare, Inc. (King of Prussia, Pennsylvania), where she was responsible for the standards of practice and professional programs and products for this company's fifty-five hundred direct-care providers in forty-two states to increase profits and enhance service quality and customer satisfaction. In 1994 she founded The Outcomes Management Group, Ltd. (Columbus, Ohio), a results-oriented international consulting company that works with a diverse clientele in both the private and public sectors.

Hicks has given more than two hundred presentations to local, state, national, and international conferences. She has published more than thirty articles and two book chapters. In 1989, in recognition of her contributions to the speech-language pathology profession, she was awarded one of the highest honors of the American Speech-Language-Hearing Association when she was selected to be a Fellow.

Hicks received her bachelor of science degree in speech-language pathology from Hampton University (Hampton, Virginia); master of arts degree in speech-language pathology from Michigan State University (East Lansing, Michigan); and doctor of philosophy degree from Memphis University (Memphis, Tennessee). Both Michigan State (1990) and Memphis University (1985) have selected her as Outstanding Alumnus of the Year.